Plant Based Cookbook for Beginners

1000 Days of Wholesome Plant-Based Diet Recipes to Cook Clean, Green and Healthy 28 Day Meal Plan Included.

Pamela Clarke

D1716598

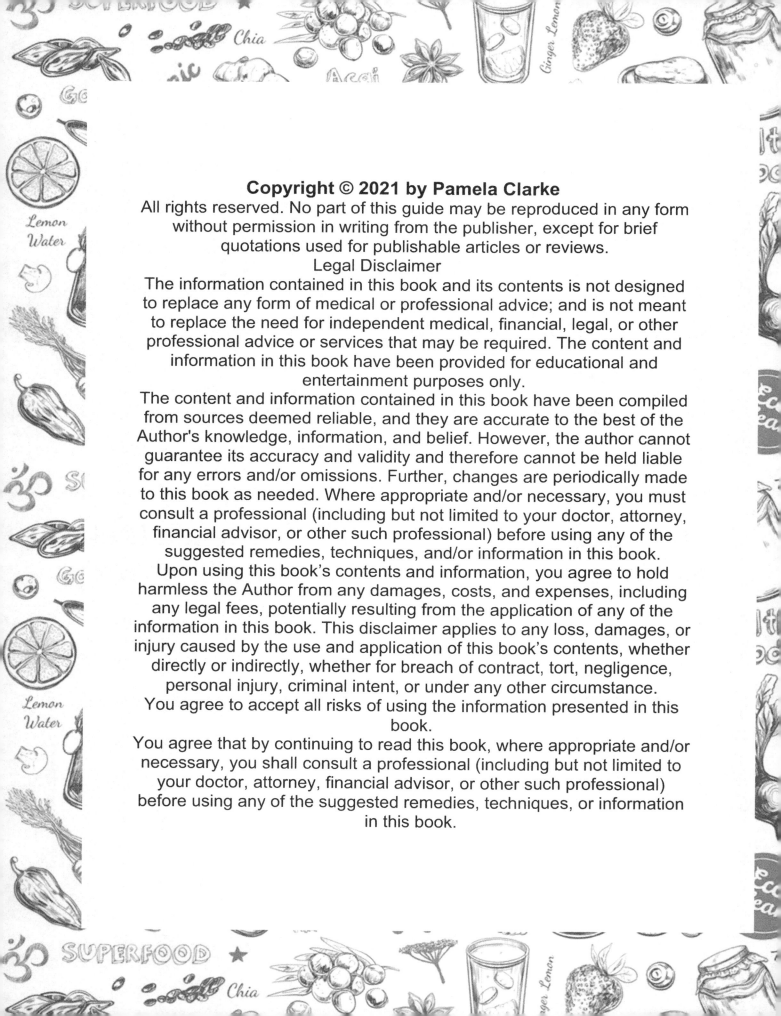

Table of Contents

Introduction

There is no magic bullet to healthy living: it is only about learning the hard truths of what you eat and what you should eat to embrace the greener side of life.

More and more people are switching to plant-based foods: celebrities, famous people, influencers, you name it.

Not only consumer trends have shown a rise in the plant industry and an increased awareness of the issues regarding animal agriculture.

But the brutal exploitation of animals for their meat and other subsidiaries just to meet our needs of protein, vitamins, and minerals has led people to find an alternative way of fulfilling necessary nutrients.

Which is definitely not by exterminating the very core of these precious species.

Consumers also realize they are not getting the healthiest forms of milk, meat, and poultry, since the majority of the products sold in the market are lab-treated and laden with preservatives, additives, and chemicals that kill the nutritional value until little to nothing remains.

And that it where a plant-based diet comes in: you can physically control what goes inside your body and can be more selective with your dietary choices. A plant-based diet is beneficial for three kinds of people.

1. Those looking forward to healthy living.
2. Those looking to lose weight.
3. Those looking to save the environment.

If you are one of them, you will enjoy this cookbook filled with a roadmap of where to get started on your plant-inspired food journey as a beginner. With 200 plant-based recipes and a 28-day meal plan to get you covered as a starting place.

Also, you will find information on common but confusing questions, basic components of a plant-based diet, both common and complex terms to familiarize with, and some smart ways of meal prepping and grocery shopping for successfully starting a plant-based diet.

CHAPTER 1: A Plant-Based Diet

What is a Plant-Based Diet?

There are many sides to a plant-based diet, which may have driven you to confusion while researching. Though, there is nothing to worry about.

A plant-based diet follows a simple formula: eat a variety of vegetables and fruits, including legumes, beans, nuts, whole grains and oils. Avoid processed foods, artificial ingredients, and limit or consume little meat and dairy depending on your preference—but never in excess.

If you are a meat lover or eat meat occasionally, it can be difficult to give up meat at first. However, plant-based eating patterns do not necessarily restrict meat or dairy consumption.

They only emphasize a diet with more plant sources and limiting artificial ingredients. Hence, with the right information and tools, anybody can make the switch.

Plant-Based Diet vs. Vegan

A plant-based diet is often confused with veganism, which is also a type of plant-based diet, hence the dread that settles over people whose meals center around meat. In a sense, vegan and plant-based diets are similar but have their fair share of differences as well.

The former is more extreme in terms of animal products, and the latter is more versatile since animal products are not off-limits.

But in the end, it all comes down to the particular person and their preferences.

Vegan

Vegan diets are stricter since there is no room for meat, eggs, milk, honey, and everything that is derived from animals.

Veganism is a way of life. It not only affects your dietary habits, but consumerism beyond food on a whole different level. The focus is on the ethics of animal cruelty, which is why it encourages consumers to avoid all products exploiting animals.

The vegan lifestyle forbids wearing clothing made from animals, such as leather and fur, as well as using products derived from animals or tested on animals. The limitations also apply to toiletries and cosmetics that include beeswax, animal fats, gelatin, silk, wool, lanolin, etc.

Plant-Based Diet

A plant-based diet only promotes healthy eating. Plant-based diet followers can eat meat and its derivatives in moderation, and as long as those are minimally processed—no chemicals, added salt and sugar, saturated fats, etc, are allowed. Essentially it is about finding ingredients and products in their most natural state.

There is no calorie or carb counting with this diet. As long as you are consuming plants and sustainable ingredients daily, you are covered for good.

A plant-based diet doesn't restrict nor ask you to resist, it just inspires you to become more mindful of your diet. It is also a lifestyle centering only around food for reversing illnesses or serious personal causes such as anxiety, depression, overweight, etc.

Because a good diet vs. a poor diet has its physical and mental impacts, which I'll outline in this book.

Types of Plant-Based Diets

There are stages to a plant-based diet which makes it so flexible for everyone's preference and lifestyle.

1. **Macrobiotic Diet:** It highlights sea vegetables, other vegetables, whole grains, beans, miso soup, and naturally processed foods. Seafood and animal products are optional.
2. **Raw Veganism:** Raw and dehydrated foods are included in this diet.
3. **Vegetarianism:** It consists of legumes, vegetables, nuts and fruit. You can eat eggs and dairy on this diet, but not meat.
4. **Veganism:** A vegan diet includes legumes, fruits, grains, vegetables, nuts, and seeds, but you can't eat any animal products.
5. **Pescatarian:** A semi-vegetarian diet that allows dairy, eggs, shellfish, and fish.
6. **Lacto Vegetarianism:** Dairy products, fruits and vegetables, but not eggs.
7. **Ovo-lacto Vegetarianism:** Eggs and dairy products along with fruits and vegetables.
8. **Ovo Vegetarianism:** Eggs with fruits and vegetables, but not dairy.
9. **Semi-Vegetarianism:** This is a mostly vegetarian diet, and occasionally you can have meat.
10. **Fruitarianism:** A fruit-based vegan diet, but this is not recommended for diabetics.
11. **Whole Foods Plant-Based Diet**: fruits and vegetables, nuts, seeds, whole grains and legumes. Avoid processed food and limit animal products, including honey, milk and eggs.

As you can see, there are different levels to a plant-based diet, harboring both a strict and simple diet philosophy.

But to eliminate any confusion, I'll only concentrate on a whole-food plant-based diet based on simple principles.

Typically, whole foods are unprocessed and derived from plants. We consume whole wheat, whole pasta, tofu, certain nuts, and non-dairy milks. But since they are seen as animal alternatives, and as long as they are minimally processed, you are on the right path. As for meat, an 80/20 split is fine, but going animal-free is always recommended.

The basic principles of a plant-based diet

- **Whole Foods:** products with little to no artificial ingredients such as whole wheat pasta, plant milk, brown bread, etc.
- **Plants:** fruits, vegetables, seeds, nuts, tofu, and legumes.
- **Avoid Animal products** as much as possible.
- **No additives or artificial flavors** such as refined foods, processed oils, added sugar and salt.
- **Herbs & Spices**: basil, mint, oregano, cardamom, iodized sea salt, etc.
- Best to approach **locally sourced, organic food** as much as possible.

I have focused on sharing plant-based recipes in this book, so you will never be short on ideas when starting this diet. Additionally, these recipes are versatile enough to allow the addition of animal-based products or meat in general, if you prefer.

Even so, I would like to convey the true essence of a plant-based diet with rich plant-based recipes. Especially if you want to stick to the original, unchanged version of this diet, these recipes will set you up for success on your way to a healthy diet.

Chapter 2: Why Should You Go Plant-Based?

Health is one of the greatest gifts of life. According to several studies, a healthy diet nourishes you from the core and promotes energy, whereas poor diet's consumers suffer from lethargy, weight gain and are more prone to developing serious illnesses compared to the former.

Don't take your health for granted. Eat healthfully! No matter how addicted you are about junk food and meat, take small steps on a healthy journey, if you have to. Because health is a matter of life and death: it is common sense!

Eating healthy in small portions or even setting yourself up for a short challenge before committing to it completely allows your body to actually understand what healthy eating feels like. This is sound advice for anyone who starts something new. As a result, you might be pleasantly surprised how positively your body reacts to a healthy diet.

I believe that people eat meat mostly because of its taste rather than nutrition.

It is fine to have your cheat days once in a while, or to divide your days by dedicating two days to meat and the rest to vegetables.

Because it is equally important to celebrate those plants that nourish our bodies from the inside out. Vegetables are available in all their tasteful and beautifully textured glory, and as humans we must appreciate all the gifts of the earth.

Even if it takes time for you to get comfortable with changing your diet, take your time. At least give it a go before adapting to it long-term. Turning over a new page takes time and commitment.

Gaining health doesn't have to be boring, you just have to find different alternatives for what you find delicious and develop your taste accordingly. If you follow the recipes in this cookbook, you will be amazed that changing your diet doesn't necessarily mean sacrificing your taste for a healthy lifestyle.

The Benefits of a Plant-Based Diet

It is easy to give advice and motivate others, but let's take the help of relevant research to guide you on the benefits of a plant-based diet, with real facts. This way you will understand why eating healthy is a matter of survival.

And the benefits of switching to a plant-based diet are plentiful.

In fact, health and wellness experts agree that a diet rich in fruits and vegetables and low on processed foods and animal products improves health and proves effective at stimulating weight loss.

It even curbs chronic diseases such as type 2 diabetes, inflammation, kidney stones, bowel diseases, heart problems, cancer, and much more.

It Controls Blood Sugar Levels

Studies have shown that people who follow a plant-based diet have a 50% lower risk of developing type 2 diabetes than those people who consume an unhealthy diet.

In a plant-based diet, a great deal of fiber is consumed, which slows the absorption of sugar into the bloodstream. It also controls blood cortisol levels that are directly involved in stress and anxiety. Also, this diet keeps you feeling fuller for longer.

It is Economical

Processed foods and animal products are costlier than fruits and vegetables. This is something you will notice as well when budgeting for a plant-based diet. It also stresses on seasonal local produce which makes it a lot more efficient and economical.

Checks Weight

Over 69% of US adults are overweight. And in over 10 studies conducted, more than 1100 people consuming plant-based diets lost 2kg over an average of 18 weeks than those who consumed non-vegetarian diets according to the researchers.

One of the main reasons to turn to a plant-based diet is it makes shedding off excess weight easier.

Not to mention, maintaining the weight becomes hassle-free without having to rely on calorie or carb restrictions, or counting for that matter.

This is because a plant-based diet is full of fiber, vitamins and minerals that work as a natural stimulant for weight loss, unlike animal fats and protein.

Improves Mood

Animal products have a high protein and fat content that your body works harder to digest. It also causes inflammation which worsens depression and leads you to be fatigued and mentally drained. A plant-based diet, on the other hand, is rich in antioxidants which slows down inflammation, thereby giving a mood boost. Some of food items known to lift your mood are beans, lentils, citrus fruits, nuts & seeds. Rolled oats, sweet potatoes and tofu that are all part of a plant-based diet.

Heart-Healthy

Studies have shown people who eat a plant-based diet have a significantly lower risk of developing heart diseases than those following non-vegetarian diets.

To be specific, a plant-based diet is low on fat and cholesterol which not only keeps your heart healthy but can reverse the effects of heart disease. Essentially, a plant-based diet free from fruit juices, sugary drinks and refined grains.

Fights Chronic Diseases

In many studies, a diet rich in vegetables and fruits have shown to prevent and improve cognitive diseases, such as Alzheimer's and dementia due to a high content of healthy plant compounds and antioxidants in a plant-based diet. This leads to a longer and healthier life as well.

Environmentally Friendly

If one of the reasons you are interested in a plant-based diet is sustainability, then know that this diet is extremely environmentally friendly. A study suggests that animal products, such as eggs, meat and dairy have a higher carbon footprint than plant-based foods.

In fact, opting for vegetables and fruits, earth-friendly foods not only support the local economy but leads to a decrease in factory farming, thus reducing water consumption, greenhouse gas emissions, less animal exploitation, and less environmental damage in particular.

Why to Cut Back On Processed Foods & Animal Products?

It is common knowledge that processed food and animal products are not safe to consume. In honesty, people, especially teenagers and young adults eat it more for the taste and the rush of dopamine, not to mention that it is seen as a quick fix too. But quick fixes rarely achieve great results.

And seeking a quick fix in food is definitely not the way to be healthy.

You might have been scolded by your mom several times for eating junk food. Because let's be frank, it is unhealthy, and according to research, there is more to it.

A western diet is brimming with preservatives, unhealthy fats, additives and whatnot: which only lead to a range of serious health issues.

Processed Foods Impact: An Overview

Let's face it, processed foods and animal-based products are loaded with harmful ingredients. Those ingredients , such as refined carbohydrates, excess sugar and high fructose corn syrup, also have highly addictive properties that can get your body addicted to these foods. Consuming them long-term can create a damaging ripple effect.

The addiction activates a feeling of satisfaction — dopamine — our brains neurotransmitter, that may give you a quick energy boost, but will leave you sluggish later. Why? Because nutritionally these foods give you nothing! And because of the taste and the feeling of serotonin may tempt you to continue eating, which can lead to issues like weight gain, calorie overconsumption, high insulin levels, depression, and accumulation of harmful chemicals that can cause other deadly illnesses.

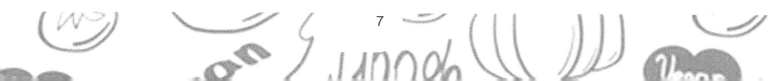

Just like a drug addict knows the killing aspect of drugs yet continues to experience that familiar intoxication, junk food eaters know that not the best is going in their stomach, yet they continue to experience that quick boost of addictive feel-good taste.

In fact, a compilation of such harmful ingredients in our body makes our system fail to differentiate between the good and bad nutrients. And the drawback of your body refusing to recognize between essential nutrients to damaging ones, from chronic diseases to muscle loss, cannot be stressed enough.

Animal-Based Products Impact: An Overview

A common concern for people who consume a plant-based diet are the plant proteins — essential amino acids, which are considered not enough compared to animal proteins. What most people don't get is that an over-consumption of essential amino acids can be quite injurious to health unlike what It is portrayed to be.

Fiber deficiency is quite common around the world. Plus, a deficiency in fiber can lead to breast and colon cancer, constipation, and more. However, in a bid to fulfill this deficiency, people rely on high animal protein intake which displaces the plant protein already existing in their bodies.

Which is bad news because unlike plant proteins, animal protein lacks in fiber, phytonutrients and antioxidants which contribute to a healthier, cancer-free body.

Animal-based products contain certain chemicals that can increase IGF-1 — a hormone insulin-like growth factor responsible for cell division and its growth. But high levels of this hormone can cause cancer cells in the body.

Given how valuable animal protein is made out to be, it is quite "dangerous". Plant protein is enough to meet your required body needs but relying on excessive animal-based products to meet the need doesn't cut it according to research.

A Plant-Based Lifestyle: The Views of Some Influential People

Let's give you an additional dose of inspiration. You might remember that in the introduction, I told you how famous people are switching to a plant-based diet, right? Well, before you form any opinions or make any assumptions, let me tell you that this is not a fad diet.

In fact, its origins go back to the 1980's, when a doctor named T. Colin Campbell introduced the plant-based diet to the world of food science. This diet stressed on low fat, high fiber and vegetable content. Back then, it wasn't associated with ethics.

Not to mention, this diet has been known in India and Israel for centuries and is an important part of Jamaican and Ethiopian cuisine.

But it wasn't long before people realized the negative effects of modern animal agriculture on plants and nature in particular.

Since then, adopting a plant-based lifestyle has become more of a responsibility for many people, including famous people who have incredible things to say about this diet. But beyond the responsibility, they realized that going plant-based is the only way to a healthy living.

Influencers and celebrities and famous personalities have an important role to play when it comes to creating awareness.

Check out what they're saying. You might spot some of your favorites talking about the diet!

Lewis Hamilton, a prominent racing driver, jumped on the vegan bandwagon due to animal cruelty and for a healthy body. This is what he said to Independent Magazine in an interview, "There is a multitude of things and I am always trying to raise the bar. One of the things was my sleeping pattern and not feeling right in the stomach. Your gut is your second brain. We're taught to drink milk and eat meat for protein, and I started looking into other areas of research around this."

Jessica Chastain, a well-known actress, has been following a plant-based diet for 10 years. This is what she told W Magazine, "Being vegan was not something I ever wanted to be. I just really was listening to what my body was telling me."

Natalie Portman, an acclaimed actress, known for various films especially "The Black Swan" has good things to say about the plant-based diet to Vanity Fair. "When I started learning about the conditions and the environmental effect of all these animals and the impact on humans of having large groups of sick animals together, it really made me want to change immediately."

Woody Harrelson, a well-known actor known for the movie "Venom" went plant-based in his 20's. He told Metro UK, "I used to eat burgers and steak, but I would just feel knocked out afterwards. I had to give them up. Dairy was first, though."

Michelle Pfeiffer turned vegetarian to stay healthy and slow down the signs of aging. This is what she said to Urbanette, "Eating a vegan diet—it is just so much healthier—and you avoid a lot of toxins that could age your skin and your body. I really noticed a difference in my skin not too long after switching to fully vegan."

Benedict Cumberbatch, a popular male actor was named "Peta's" Most Beautiful Vegan. Given the actor's tiptop shape, no wonder he credits a plant-based diet for all his health and fine looks.

Common Concerns with a Plant-Based Diet

To avoid meat in a plant-based diet is not a compulsion, but It is better if you don't make it a central part of your diet — more of a garnishing piece instead. You just have to gradually ease into it, until you feel that your body can accept going plant-based fully.

Because of the low meat and animal-based product intake, many individuals have questions regarding protein, calcium and B12 deficiency regarding this diet. And there are those who dislike certain foods or are allergic to some ingredients. In that case, I recommend you read the following advice.

What If You don't like Certain Foods or are Allergic?

Well, for starters, a plant-based diet is not known for its restrictions, but rather for the flexibility it provides. For example, if you don't like soy or are allergic to peanut butter, don't consume them. Simply turn to their alternatives. In the case of peanut butter, choose other nut butters. As for soy, tempeh, miso, tofu and edamame, which are also less processed do the job. Though, consult a dietician about adding soy to your diet for protein if you've undergone breast cancer or thyroid disease, because there are concerns about plant estrogens in soy. However, research has found that taking soy in moderation is safe for other people.

Essential Nutrients

Let's be frank, people are obsessed with protein — those are the building blocks in your body that take care of your hormones, bones, blood, and tissues. But due to a lot of misinformation, people think it is only found in meat. But that is not how the nutritionists put it. A daily intake of protein should be 56 grams in men and 46 grams in women. I am not saying that there are plant proteins that are inefficient, but there are good substitutes to meat protein found in brown rice, quinoa, nuts, beans, lentils and buckwheat that fit the bill.

Protein deficiency is rare unless someone's extremely malnourished. With a regular intake of protein-rich plant-based foods, you can easily achieve your required protein fix.

Calcium

Okay, let's come down to calcium. Which is also a concerning factor for those starting a plant-based diet. Plant sources of calcium are often regarded with suspicion, but once again, but plant-information wise, something is amiss. Because ingredients like broccoli, kale, and almonds are excellent sources of calcium.

Vitamin B12 Deficiency

It is a major concern for people who follow a plant-based diet. Fortified plant-based milks and whole-grain cereals make up for that. So, the key here is to find fortified products and take a B12 vitamin supplement to meet your daily dose of 2.4 mg. Take B12-rich foods in small amounts throughout the day, not all at once. For further guidance on this, I recommend that you consult your doctor or health-care provider before starting a new diet or supplementation.

As for the rest of important minerals, vitamins, and antioxidants, following a healthy plant-based diet religiously will take care of that.

Healthy Fats & Carbohydrates

The Mayo Clinic recommends 225-325 g of carbs per day. Carbs are the primary source of energy for a healthy, nourished body, regardless of how popular no-carb diets are. Then there is the case of simple and complex carbs. Simple carbs can include processed foods that offer no nutrition: they're just empty calories.

While some simple carbs with a high fiber content are found in fruits and vegetables which are super-healthy for a properly functioning body. Quinoa, oatmeal, and brown rice are complex carbs that keep you feeling full for longer periods of time. They should be an important addition to your diet.

Fats are shunned just as carbs are, but not all fats are unhealthy. You need some of those good fats for a healthy metabolism and fewer "hangry" moments. Many sources recommend that fats should make up 20-30% of your daily calories, but there is also talk regarding the type of fats you should consume.

Extra-virgin olive oil, oats, nuts, seeds, avocados, and nut butters make up some of the good fats. Whereas bad fats are saturated and trans fats found in processed foods and animal-based products which can lead to serious illnesses like cardiovascular issues in the long run. So make up your mind about how to approach carbs and fats as part of a healthy, plant-based diet.

Chapter 3: How to Adopt a Plant-Based Lifestyle?

Some people mistakenly believe that switching to a plant-based diet will automatically make them healthier. The biggest mistake you can make in this journey is blindly trusting product labels and certain so-called industry-touted, plant-based and ready-made foods such as plant-based junk foods, non-dairy ice creams and frozen veggie pizzas as healthy.

A plant-based diet has its benefits, but you can't expect that everything will be at your disposal from the get-go. It is more about finding connection with natural ingredients and foods, even if that means growing your own ingredients or cooking your own healthy meals from scratch.

As a result, you will completely mislead yourself if you think that consuming these artificially made yet plant-based foods daily will help you achieve your health goals: in fact, it will harm them.

It is true that these foods keep you motivated; hence, there is a reason why cheat days exist. However, they're not the best route to take when adopting a plant-based lifestyle and should be consumed in moderation.

Therefore, it is important to educate yourself thoroughly on the foods you should eat and stock, those you should eat sparingly and stock to some degree, and those you should completely avoid.

Having said that, let's move on to the fun part: pantry stocking and making your plant-based diet success a dream come true!

Make Up Your Mind About Plant-Based Eating

What does a plant-based diet mean to you? More importantly, how do you see yourself pursuing this diet? You should ask these questions at the very beginning, so you can customize the diet based on your lifestyle and commitment.

In this regard, you cannot alter or adapt the diet to unhealthy means as it would be of no use to follow a diet that still adheres to your old ways that you desperately wish to shed.

However, if going plant-based means that you give up artificial foods and meat gradually, then you are on the right track. Just don't forget to keep the foods you should be eating a majority in your new diet.

Plant-Based Food Analysis

Let's talk about the types of foods that you will be eating now that we have your mindset in place. Beginners may be surprised by the number of vegan products available on the market, and they will be much keener on reading the labels and claims.

However, not all the information you read is accurate. It is no secret that plant-based diets are a big thing, especially for food industry giants and marketers, but instead of getting sucked in all fancy jargon, colorful product titles and other marketing techniques that justify the existence of these products as being "plant-based" actually hides a lot of animal derivatives you need to avoid.

Even if you still want to consume some animal-based food including pre-packaged foods, you must be vigilant about the loaded fats, sodium, sugar, preservatives, additives and other things that can negatively impact your diet.

Take Your Time

As with any hobby, don't rush into things. Start slowly. We're eager to get started with something new, but our energy wanes as soon as we feel bored with it. In particular, if you are a meat lover and enjoy comfort foods from time to time, try revamping these recipes with plant-based recipes so you won't feel deprived.

As an example:

If you crave a chicken burger, why not swap the chicken for mushrooms instead and create your own veggie burger? It will take some time for your taste buds to adjust to these new flavors, textures, and seasonings, but it will be worth it in the end.

You might like to try zucchini noodles instead of pasta or tofu cubes instead of kebabs. Vegetables can be prepared in so many ways, and I've outlined some impressive and easy recipes in this cookbook that you will forget even your favorite non-vegetarian dishes.

Do Your Research & Follow Like-Minded People

The transition to a healthier lifestyle or the creation of new habits can be difficult, especially when done alone. You could simplify it by following like-minded people during your journey. You can also discuss and share your problems with friends or others who inspired you to follow a plant-based diet: seasoned vegans will have much to share with beginners like you. In times when you crave junk food, feel like giving up, or cannot understand something, they may motivate you.

Marci Shimoff's quote captures it best:

"It is support that sustains us on the journey we've started."

To help you on your plant-based journey, I recommend that you join relevant facebook groups, Pinterest group boards, Quora and reddit forums. Educate yourself by following trusted industry experts of plant-based diets who actually follow this diet like It is projected to be.

Alternatively, if you don't have time, this cookbook will get you started in the right direction because it covers everything a beginner might need to know or the common struggles they might encounter.

An Overview of Pantry Planning

We all deserve a fresh start, especially when turning a new page. Any recollections or reminders of your past habits can discourage you from your goals and pose an unhealthy invitation to forgo current goals or achievements, for that matter.

Thus, I would recommend that you purge your kitchen before you start, as it may eliminate temptations from your previous diet. You need to get rid of all junk foods, processed foods, dairy, eggs, and meat as well as condiments, sauces, and dressings in your refrigerator as those may contain a host of artificial and chemical ingredients you need to avoid.

The Purge

You might have a hard time doing this, but I promise you it will be worth it in the long run as you will be setting the stage for a range of delicious foods to enjoy. To begin, you must understand that you are not sacrificing taste, you are giving up old, unhealthy habits. If you are worried about food waste, donate any edibles to your local food bank. Ask your friends, family, and neighbors whether they would like to have any of the products you are getting rid of that are within the expiration dates. By doing so, you will avoid food waste.

Filling The Food Pantry

If you purge your kitchen, you may have a pretty bare pantry, drawers, and cupboards, but no worries: you will soon have a fresh, well-organized and colorful pantry filled with ingredients and foods that are tailored specifically for your health goals.

In this diet, you don't have to worry about stocking, as the local farmer's market will have what you need but if you want to keep everything on hand, you can buy them in bulk at your local grocery stores.

- **Refrigerator:** It is useful to purchase in advance all fruits for your fridge. This cookbook includes many recipes that call for various kinds of fruit. For more information, please refer to the diet guide.
- **Freezer:** All the frozen goods go in your freezer. These include frozen fruits and vegetables. Consult the diet guide for a shopping list.
- **Pantry:** All your canned and dry goods go here, including nuts, seeds, oils, legumes, whole grains, and herbs.

Organization:

You should not stock your kitchen blindly. Create a menu so you don't have to make meals decisions every day and organize everything to keep a clear head.

The 28-day meal plan including 200 recipes in this cookbook are ideal as they can be personalized according to your needs and choosing a meal plan for every day will make you never run out of great vegetables and fruits, and cooking ideas.

To give every ingredient a home, buy transparent containers, jars, baskets, and kitchen organizing supplies. As a result, you will have easy access to and be able to spot everything while cooking and will set yourself up for success in the long run.

Kitchen Essentials:

An assortment of cutlery, serving bowls, utensils, strainers, whisks, and tongs is necessary. You should also check which accessories you can afford and which you can do without or substitute. While this list of must-haves will cover you, if you want to omit some or have a better alternative, use it instead.

I recommend purchasing a sharp knife and a good cutting board. You will be slicing and dicing a lot. It will be lifesaving to have a razor-sharp knife in your arsenal along with a solid cutting board to practice on. Not to mention, time-saving too!

Can Opener
Yes, you will need a can opener to open all the food cans, and it will be very handy.

Measuring Cups & Spoons
Having a standard set of measuring cups & spoons is essential for all baking recipes.

Pots, pans & baking dishes
Cooking plant-based foods requires large pots, woks, skillets, saucepans, and oven-safe baking dishes. You may also need rimmed baking sheets.

Silicone Spatula & Mixing bowls
Unlike plastic, silicone spatulas are exceptionally heat-resistant making them super-helpful for baking, mixing, sauteing and you will need them all the time while cooking. Same is the case with mixing bowls. For tossing and combining ingredients, you should have a few mixing bowls to prepare food.

Food Processor & Blender
Almost all of the foods in a plant-based diet are homemade, even some condiments. Making sauces, dips, condiments, soups, and so much more requires a convenient and fast blender or food processor.

Toaster Oven/Microwave With A Baking Option
Toaster oven is important for baking, and you should have one if you want to try the baking recipes in this cookbook.

Food Containers
These are useful for food leftovers, so you should have a good collection of food boxes.

Hand blender/Immersion Blender
It is easier to mash food with a hand blender, particularly when whipping up soups and stews.

Pressure Cooker/Multi Cooker
This is a great way to cook batch meals or food that takes a while to soften, like beans and grains.

A Nut Milk Bag/Cheesecloth
Making and straining nut milks requires either of these!

Diet Guide for Going Plant-Based

The following diet guide serves as a shopping list for your plant-based diet. Having these ingredients in stock will ensure you can try any recipe in this book.

Foods To Stock

Starchy Vegetables	Non-starchy Vegetables	Fruits	Whole Grains	Beverages
All kinds of potatoes, sweet potatoes, etc.	Leafy greens: lettuce, kale, spinach, etc	All kinds of fruit, even frozen fruits for convenience. No dried fruits or fruit juices included.	Brown rice, whole wheat paste, whole-grain products	Water,
All legumes: lentils, peas, chickpeas and beans	Broccoli	Apples, bananas, citrus fruits	Barley, rolled oats,	Green tea
Root vegetables	Zucchini, cabbage	Pineapples, peaches, avocados	Brown rice pasta, whole-grain breads	Unsweetened plant milks
Root corn	Eggplants, carrots, cauliflower,	Berries, pears	Farro	Decaffeinated coffee
Quinoa	Tomatoes, onions, garlic, ginger, etc	Watermelon, etc	Buckwheat	Decaffeinated tea

Spices	Omega-3 Sources	Nuts & Nut Butters	Condiments	Seasonings
All spices	Ground flax seeds	Peanuts	Soy sauce	Thyme
Black pepper, cayenne pepper, chili powder, curry powder	Chia seeds	Almonds	Lemon juice	Basil
Ground cinnamon, turmeric, ground cumin, onion powder, garlic powder	Kidney beans	Cashews	Vinegar	Rosemary, cilantro, mint
Nutritional yeast, red	Hemp seeds	Walnuts	Mustard	Curry powder

pepper flakes				
Italian seasoning	Edamame	Macadamia nuts	Salsa	Sea salt

Foods To Eat In Moderation

Dried Fruits
Coconuts
Avocados
Seeds: sunflower seeds, pumpkin seeds, sesame seeds
Beverages: alcoholic drinks, decaffeinated tea & coffee
Added Sweeteners: maple syrup, fruit juice concentrate, natural sugars
Refined Protein: Wheat protein, wheat gluten protein, soy protein isolate, tofu

Foods To Avoid

Meat	Dairy	Added Fats	Beverages
Fish	Yogurt	Liquid Oils	Fruit Juice
Poultry	Milk	Coconut Oil	Energy Drinks
Seafood	Cheese	Margarine	Sports Drinks
Red meat	Cream	Butter	Soda
Processed Meat	Buttermilk	Peanut Oil	Coffee & tea blends

Fast Food	Refined Grains	Added Sugars	Processed Foods
Cheeseburgers	White rice	Pastries	Cakes

French fries	White bread	Bakery goods	Cereal bars
Nuggets	White pasta	Cereals	Frozen dinners
Pizza	Bagels	Cookies	Quick mixes
Hot dogs	Crackers	Candies	Bacon, beef jerky, sausage

Plant-based Alternatives

Non-Plant-Based Foods	**Plant-Based Foods Alternatives**
Eggs	Applesauce, flaxseed eggs, mashed banana, tofu, etc
Milk	Unsweetened plant-based milks; almond, soy, coconut, hemp, etc
Cheese	Nutritional yeast, sliced avocado, sprouted organic tofu, soaked and blended cashews
Meat	Tempeh, tofu, portobello mushrooms, chickpeas, cauliflower, veggie burgers, walnuts, lentils, jackfruit
Butter	Extra-virgin olive oil, tahini, coconut oil, avocado oil, applesauce
Honey	Raw date paste, maple syrup
Yogurt	Plain plant-based yogurt; soy, almond, cashew, oat
Cheese Sauce	Plant-based queso dip
Egg whites	Aquafaba

Words of Advice

Plant-based diets exist solely for the purpose of encouraging clean eating. When you don't understand the food journey you are on, there is no need to rush into things and make unfortunate mistakes. When buying plant-based foods, you might be tempted by the labels, and here are the eight products that are most suspicious when following a plant-based diet correctly.

I believe you should avoid anything that sounds suspicious. Check out the following as they'll help you make an informed decision and avoid any blunders.

Bread

Most breads contain dairy products, so they are not plant-based. For those of you who cannot give up sliced bread, you can make your own plant-based bread at home. Even though it will take more time and effort, it'll be worth it and a healthy, better tasting alternative in the end.

Vegetable Stock

Be aware of the fact that even "mock" chicken stocks may contain trace amounts of animal derivatives or animal fat. Vegan stocks also fall under this category, so be cautious! Rather, make it yourself instead.

Dairy-Free Cheese

It is possible to find nondairy cheeses made from soy, nuts, or rice, but they may contain whey protein or casein. If you are searching for a cheese substitute, you should look for a vegan label.

Pasta

A key component of pasta are eggs, so make sure you buy only dried pasta. Make sure the pasta is made with whole grains as well as water.

Non-dairy Creamer

It is possible that creamers don't include milk, but they often do such as milk proteins like sodium caseinate. Find vegan-friendly creamers instead

Orange Juice

Fish oil is found in most orange juices. Fish oil may be good for you, but it may go against a plant-based diet especially if you are following a whole-foods type.

Granola

The ingredients are usually dried fruits, nuts, seeds, and raw grains. Butter and sugar are often added as well. Ideally, you should make your own.

Vegan Sausages & Burgers

Most of these products contain eggs or milk, so they are not entirely plant-based. There is also a possibility that they contain a lot of soy, so be careful which ones you purchase. For anyone who is concerned about what's going into it, they can make their own.

Simple Ways to Make Plant-Based Meals More Flavorful

As I have mentioned many times in the book, following a plant-based diet does not mean sacrificing your taste for health. Instead, It is about finding inspiration and discovering all the wonderful vegetables and fruits that are available to us, which unfortunately, lives under a shadow because of the popularity of meat, hence most of us are unaware.

The right ingredients can do a splendid job of bringing up the flavors of these vegetables and fruits. Listed below are the three things you should not forget when preparing quick veggie meals; they will allow their flavors and colors to shine!

Olive & Coconut Oil: Healthy fats can keep you fuller for longer and can enhance the taste and texture of a meal. In addition to having no trans fats, extra-virgin olive oil is great for roasting and searing. In addition, the moistness and creaminess of coconut oil is ideal for baking.

Herbs Enhance Flavor: Adding fresh or dried herbs to food adds flavor without added burden of calories or sodium. My personal favorite herbs are cilantro, mint, rosemary, and parsley.

Spices: The spices are critical when creating plant-based dishes, and you should check out our diet guide to see the kind of spices you must have in stock. A variety of spices, including turmeric, curry powder, cinnamon, garlic, and ginger can increase the flavor and spiciness of food.

Sweeteners: Sweetening food with unrefined sugar is the way to go; they're much safer and easier alternatives to traditional sugar. I highly recommend maple syrup and dates.

Labels: What You Might Want To Know

There is no portion control in a plant-based diet. You can eat whenever you like and whenever you feel hungry. It is important that you realize that food consumption should be based on products that provide you with energy from the inside out, and this happens only if you consume a fresh, healthy and natural diet, which is free of animal-based products and packaged foods.

When stocking your kitchen and pantry, It is important not to purchase foods that require a lot of packaging or labels. Occasionally, you will need to purchase a packaged food item. Here are a few tips you can use when situations like this arise so you can stay vigilant and participate in a healthy shopping experience.

Beware of Company Claims

Frequently, packaged food includes terms like '50% less sodium' or 'low in fat'. However, these terms do not actually hold any significant meaning. Instead of focusing on the attention-grabbing labels, you should concentrate on the ingredients and nutritional information. There is no guarantee a pack of crackers will be healthy just because it contains less sodium than others. It could still be high in sodium and even contain other negative ingredients. The same is true for low-fat products.

Always Check Ingredients
The less the ingredients, the healthier the food is; that's the rule of thumb you need to stick by. Many of such foods are low in additives and preservatives, making them healthier food choices. If anything, it is a good indicator that a food contains a lot of sugar if there are a lot of ingredients ending in "-ose." In addition, make sure the ingredient list does not contain any animal products.

How to Make It a Success?

Be Optimistic

Maintaining a plant-based diet and achieving your health and fitness goals are easier when you maintain a positive attitude. While this demands diligence and dedication, having a positive outlook and mindset is important for staying motivated, focusing on the positive aspects of your diet, and overcoming negative emotions.

Improve Water Intake

Water helps you keep your appetite in check. Drinking a glass of water suppresses the artificial feeling of hunger, helping you lose weight and supporting fat metabolism. As water is calorie, fat, cholesterol, and low in sodium, it is your best friend when it comes to staying fit inside and out.

Consume A Lot Of Fiber

The benefits of eating lots of dietary fiber are numerous. And some of the important ones are regulating bowel health and movements, controlling blood cholesterol levels, balancing blood sugar levels and encouraging a healthier gut, while also reducing the risk of serious complications such as cancer.

Work Out

Exercising regularly and being physically active has numerous health benefits. Taking regular exercise can help you control weight, combat illnesses, improve mood, boost energy, and sleep better, and you start to experience the changes from the first week, so what are you waiting for?

Never Skip Sleep

As you strive for a healthy lifestyle, sleep and rest will become increasingly important. Rest and sleep are indispensable. Among its numerous benefits are appetite control, calorie reduction, increased resting metabolism, and prevention of insulin resistance. Lastly, it gives you energy to exercise, which is important with the kind of healthy foods you will be eating, you have to allow your body to utilize them properly.

Be Careful When Dining Out

Eating out is difficult when you are following a plant-based diet and trying to reduce your oil and other concentrated ingredients intake. Meanwhile, the temptation of ordering takeaways and dining-in is quite strong when you've spent a strenuous day outside and cooking is simply not in the cards. So, here are some tips you should follow when eating out:

1. Look for plant-based or restaurants that serve vegan food
2. Let us know how you want your meals prepared. Steamed, baked, water sautéed, or grilled foods should be on the priority list.
3. Be kind to the waiting staff and don't be shy of making your preference known.

Chapter 4: Breakfast

1. Yummy Jelly & Peanut Butter Oatmeal

Preparation Time: 2 minutes
Cooking Time: 5 minutes
Servings: 1

Ingredients:

1. ½ cup gluten-free oats
2. 1 mashed banana
3. 1 tablespoon peanut butter
4. 1 tablespoon raspberry jelly
5. ½ teaspoon ground cinnamon
6. ½ cup with 1 tablespoon unsweetened vanilla almond milk
7. 1-s tablespoon ground flax seed

Directions:

- Put oats, ½ cup almond milk, cinnamon, and mashed banana in a small-sized saucepan.
- Turn the heat on medium flame and stir for 3-5 minutes.
- Within a few minutes, the oats will thicken and the milk will evaporate.
- After the milk has evaporated, add that 1 tablespoon of almond milk.
- Stir until the almond milk has also evaporated.
- Then transfer the oats to a bowl after taking them off the stove.
- Serve with peanut butter and jelly.

Nutrition:

Calories: 354
Protein: 10 g
Fiber: 9 g
Carbohydrates: 49 g
Sugar: 10 g
Sodium: 134 mg
Fat: 16 g
Saturated Fat: 2 g
Cholesterol: 0 mg

2. Healthy Strawberry & Coconut Smoothie

Preparation Time: 5 minutes
Cooking Time: 2 minutes
Servings: 1

Ingredients:

1. ½ cup plain greek yogurt
2. ½ cup coconut milk
3. 1 cup frozen & mildly thawed strawberries
4. 1 sliced & frozen ripe banana
5. 1 tablespoon chia seeds
6. 1 teaspoon lime juice
7. Crushed or ice cubes as needed

Directions:

- Add all the ingredients to a blender or smoothie maker.
- Process everything until smooth.
- Garnish with extra strawberries or serve immediately.

Nutrition:

Calories: 278
Protein: 14 Grams
Carbs: 57 Grams
Fat: 2 Grams

3. Sweet Potatoes With A Twist

Preparation Time: 5 minutes
Cooking Time: 10 minutes
Servings: 2

Ingredients:

1. 2 tablespoons plain vegan yogurt
2. 2 medium-sized sweet potatoes
3. 2 tablespoons almond butter
4. 2 tablespoons maple syrup
5. ½ cup homemade or store-bought granola

Directions:

1. Add all Clean the sweet potatoes thoroughly and poke holes in them with a fork.
2. Microwave them for 2 minutes, turn over to the other side and microwave

again. When done, it should be easy to pierce with a fork.

3. Let them cool.
4. Cut from the middle, make sure the insides are facing upward, and slightly mash the insides with a fork until a small mouth forms
5. Fill it with almond butter, yogurt, maple syrup and granola on top.
6. Serve hot.

Nutrition:
Calories: 410
Protein: 9g
Fiber: 8g
Fat: 16g
Carbohydrates: 62g
Sodium: 160mg

4. Gluten-Free Blueberry Pancakes
Preparation Time: 5 minutes
Cooking Time: 10 minutes
Servings: 2
Ingredients:
- ½ cup frozen or fresh blueberries
- 1 cup gluten-free flour
- 1 teaspoon apple cider vinegar
- 1 cup sugar-free plant-based milk
- 3 tablespoons maple syrup
- 1 teaspoon vanilla essence
- 1 tablespoon baking powder
- ½ teaspoon salt
- 1 tablespoon coconut oil
- 1 tablespoon extra virgin olive oil

Directions:
1. Pour milk and apple cider vinegar into a blender. Set aside for 3 minutes to make a substitute buttermilk.
2. Blend the buttermilk by adding maple syrup, olive oil and vanilla essence until smooth.
3. Next, add in flour, baking powder, and salt. Beat everything until batter forms.
4. Place a pan or griddle over medium heat and melt coconut oil.
5. Check to see if the pan is hot. Place the batter on it to make 3-inch thick

pancakes, and keep 1-inch distance between the pancakes.
6. As the pancakes are cooking, place blueberries on top of them.
7. Cook the pancakes from both sides for 3-5 minutes, or until brown.
8. Serve hot with extra maple syrup.

Nutrition:
Calories: 565
Protein: 16g
Carbohydrates: 87g
Fat: 20g
Fiber:9g
Sodium: 718mg

5. Gluten-Free Banana Oat Muffins
Preparation Time: 5 minutes
Cooking Time: 19 minutes
Servings: 10
Ingredients:
- 1 pasture-raised egg or applesauce
- ½ cup maple syrup
- 2 cup gluten-free oats
- 4 tablespoons melted coconut oil
- 1 ½ teaspoons cinnamon
- 1 teaspoon vanilla essence
- 1 teaspoon baking soda
- ½ teaspoon nutmeg
- 4 mashed bananas
- ¼ teaspoon salt

Directions:
1. Preheat oven to 350°F and transfer oats to a blender, grinder or food processor.
2. Grind until oats form a flour consistency.
3. In a separate bowl, add thoroughly mashed bananas, coconut oil, vanilla essence, egg, and maple syrup.
4. Mix all together with a fork.
5. Using a spatula, put powdered oats, nutmeg, salt, cinnamon, and baking soda.
6. Combine all the fluid and dry ingredients together properly.
7. Line the muffin tray with cupcake liners or grease them with oil.

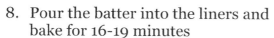

8. Pour the batter into the liners and bake for 16-19 minutes
9. Insert a toothpick, if it comes out clean, your muffins are done.
10. Let them cool and serve them after.

Nutrition:
Calories: 138
Carbohydrates: 22 g
Saturated Fat: 4 g
Sodium: 105 mg
Protein: 2 g
Sugar: 13 g
Fat: 6 g
Fiber: 2 g
Cholesterol: 16 mg

6. Breakfast Chia Seeds Chocolate Pudding
Preparation Time: 10 minutes
Cooking time:
Servings: 2
Ingredients:
- 2 medium-sized ripe & mashed bananas
- ½ cup chia seeds
- 1 tablespoon maple syrup
- ½ teaspoon vanilla essence
- 2 cups unsweetened almond milk or coconut milk
- 4 tablespoons raw cacao powder
- ½ teaspoon cinnamon

Directions:
1. Combine the dry ingredients in a large bowl and whisk.
2. Add mashed banana, maple syrup, almond milk and vanilla extract to the dry ingredients.
3. Using a whisk, mix everything well together.
4. Then cover the bowl and leave it in the fridge for 2 hours. Or better, leave overnight.
5. This will thicken up the breakfast pudding.
6. Once the pudding has thickened, blend it in a blender until smooth. (This is an optional step.
7. Serve with nuts or eat as it is.

Nutrition:
Calories: 172
Carbohydrates: 22.1 g
Protein: 4.7 g
Fat: 7.8 g
Saturated Fat: 0.8 g
Sodium: 91 mg
Potassium: 272 mg
Fiber: 8.3 g
Sugar: 9.2 g

7. Nutritional Tofu Scramble
Preparation Time: 5 minutes
Cooking Time: 10 minutes
Servings: 2
Ingredients:
- 2 tablespoons plant-based milk
- 1 tablespoon extra-virgin olive oil
- ¼ teaspoon garlic powder
- ¼ teaspoon turmeric
- 2 tablespoons nutritional yeast
- 1 16-ounce firm tofu block
- ½ teaspoon salt or as needed

Directions:
1. Set the pan over medium heat and heat olive oil.
2. Using a potato masher or your hands, mash the chunk of tofu in the pan.
3. Stir tofu occasionally until the water has evaporated.
4. Add the dry ingredients to the pan now, stirring as you go for at least 5 minutes.
5. Stir the plant-based milk into the pan.
6. Serve hot with green vegetables if you like.

Nutrition:
Calories: 288
Carbohydrates: 9g
Protein: 24g
Potassium: 168mg
Fiber: 4g
Sugar: 1g
Fat: 18g
Saturated fat: 2g
Sodium: 600mg

8. Fresh Avocado Toast With Pesto

Preparation Time: 15 minutes
Cooking Time: 15 minutes
Servings: 1

Ingredients:

- 1 Slice Gluten-Free Bread
- ⅓-¼ ripe and peeled large avocado
- ½ slices tomato
- 2 cups fresh stemless basil
- 1 tablespoon lemon juice
- 1 tablespoon extra-virgin olive oil
- 2-3 large & peeled garlic cloves
- 1 tablespoon nutritional yeast
- ¼ teaspoon sea salt and as needed
- 1 tablespoon water
- 1 pinch red chili flakes

Directions:

1. To start making pesto, add basil, lemon juice, garlic, nutritional yeast and sea salt in the blender. Pulse until a slightly runny paste forms.
2. Add olive oil and water to the mix. Use a spatula to scrape the sides and make sure a paste-like pesto forms.
3. Take your slice of bread and toast it in the toaster.
4. Apply avocado to the toast by mashing it first.
5. Serve with two tablespoons of pesto and fresh tomatoes on top of avocado.
6. Sprinkle red chili flakes and sea salt as per taste.
7. The leftover pesto can be refrigerated for 1 week.

Nutrition:

Calories: 221
Carbohydrates: 23 g
Protein: 9.1 g
Fat: 11.4 g
Saturated Fat: 1.6 g
Potassium: 512 mg
Fiber: 6.5 g
Cholesterol: 0 mg
Sodium: 438 mg

9. Crunchy Almond Cereal Breakfast

Preparation Time: 5
Cooking Time: 15
Servings: 8

Ingredients:

- 1 cup organic oats
- 1 cup organic spelt flakes
- ¼ cup date syrup
- 1 ½ cups roughly chopped almonds
- 7 tablespoons melted coconut oil
- Any plant-based milk

Directions:

1. Preheat your oven to 330 degrees Fahrenheit.
2. Line the baking tray with butter paper.
3. Add all the ingredients in a large bowl and mix it all together with a spatula.
4. The ingredients should stick together like granola bars
5. Spread the mixture onto the baking tray.
6. Bake for 15 minutes or until they become crunchy.
7. Let it cool and then break it into cereal-like pieces.
8. Serve with almond milk or any of your choice.

Nutrition:

Calories: 286
Fat: 14.7g
Carbs: 34.4g
Protein: 6.6g

10. Red Pepper Hash Browns

Preparation Time: 15 minutes
Cooking Time: 30 minutes
Servings: 5

Ingredients:

- ¾ teaspoon red pepper
- 2 tablespoons extra-virgin olive oil
- 6 ½ cups of diced potatoes
- Black pepper to taste
- Sea salt as needed
- 1 teaspoon paprika
- ¾ chili powder

Directions:

1. Turn on your oven to 400.

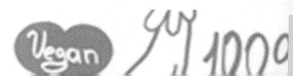

2. Take a large bowl and combine olive oil, red pepper, black pepper, sea salt and chili powder.
3. Mix together your olive oil with all the dry ingredients.
4. After coating your potatoes with the mixture, arrange them on the baking tray.
5. Put them in the oven for 30 minutes or until the potatoes are baking.
6. Let them cool down a bit and enjoy them in your breakfast.

Nutrition:
Calories: 227
Protein: 3.9 Grams
Carbs: 41.3 Grams
Fat: 5.7 Grams

11. Delicious Quinoa & Apple Breakfast Porridge

Preparation Time: 5 minutes
Cooking Time: 20 minutes
Servings: 2

Ingredients:
- 1 cup any unsweetened plant-based milk
- ¼ teaspoon cinnamon
- 1 teaspoon vanilla essence
- ⅛ teaspoon cardamom
- 1 chopped large apple
- ½ cup dry quinoa
- 1 tablespoon coconut oil
- 2 tablespoons unsweetened raisins
- A pinch of sea salt

Directions:
1. Rinse the quinoa well in a sieve to remove debris and "saponins," the outer layer that contributes to bitterness.
2. Combine rinsed quinoa with milk, cinnamon, cardamom, vanilla extract, raisins, and sea salt in a saucepan. Incorporate well.
3. Bring milk in the saucepan to a boil over high heat.
4. Reduce the heat and cover the pan once it begins to boil.

5. Simmer for 15 minutes, or until all liquid has been absorbed.
6. Let the steam sit with the lid for a couple of minutes after turning off the heat.
7. In a separate pan, heat coconut oil over medium heat while the quinoa cooks.
8. Transfer the apple chunks to the coconut oil and sprinkle cinnamon.
9. Mix well and allow to simmer for approximately 10 minutes, until lightly browned and tender.
10. Mix occasionally so that they're evenly brown.
11. Top quinoa with sautéed apples and serve in bowls.
12. You may add any additional toppings you like or extra milk.

Nutrition:
Calories: 485
Carbohydrates: 42g
Calcium: 50mg
Protein: 9g
Fat: 33g
Saturated Fat: 28g
Potassium: 582mg
Fiber: 7g
Sugar: 10g
Vitamin C: 3mg
Sodium: 168mg

12. Banana Cocoa Smoothie

Preparation Time: 10 minutes
Cooking Time: 10 minutes
Servings: 2

Ingredients:
- 3 cups plain and unsweetened plant-based yogurt
- ¼ organic peanut butter or any nut butter
- 2 teaspoons unsweetened cocoa powder
- 3 frozen & sliced bananas
- 1 cup frozen cauliflower florets
- 2 teaspoons maple syrup

Directions:
1. Add all the ingredients in a blender or your favorite smoothie-maker.
2. Blend everything until smooth
3. Serve in glasses with extra toppings of banana.

Nutrition:
Calories: 583
Fat: 24g
Carbohydrates: 79g
Protein: 23g
Fiber: 10g
Sodium: 210mg

13. Healthy Buckwheat Crepes
Preparation Time: 10 minutes
Cooking Time: 15 minutes
Servings: 12
Ingredients:
- ¾ tablespoon flaxseed meal
- 1 cup roasted raw buckwheat
- 1 ¾ cups light coconut milk
- 1 tablespoon avocado or coconut oil
- 1 pinch sea salt
- Granola or nut butter (optional)

Directions:
1. Add coconut milk, buckwheat flour, sea salt, avocado oil and flaxseed to a bowl.
2. You can do this in a blender too.
3. Whisk the ingredients until a not too thick and not too thin batter forms.
4. Put a pan or skillet on medium heat.
5. Add coconut oil and check to see if It is hot.
6. Add 60ml of batter on the pab. It should start to bubble and the sides to feel dry much like cooking pancakes.
7. Carefully flip the crepe to the other side, let it cook for 2-3 minutes.
8. Serve hot on a plate with nut butter or granola if you like.

Nutrition:
Calories: 71
Carbohydrates: 8 g
Protein: 1 g
Fat: 3 g
Saturated Fat: 3 g

Cholesterol: 0 mg
Sodium: 28 mg
Potassium: 62 mg
Fiber: 1 g
Calcium: 6 mg
Iron: 0.5 mg

14. Gluten-Free Chocolate Chip Muffins
Preparation Time: 15 minutes
Cooking Time: 28 minutes
Servings: 10
Ingredients
- ¾ cup applesauce
- ⅓ cup coconut sugar
- ¼ cup maple syrup
- 1 teaspoon baking powder
- ¼ teaspoon sea salt
- ¼ melted coconut oil
- ¼ cup unsweetened almond milk
- ½ cup unsweetened cocoa powder
- 1 ½, teaspoon baking soda
- ¾ cup gluten-free flour blend
- ⅓ cup almond flour
- ¼ cup ground rolled oat flour
- ⅓ cup dairy-free semi-sweet chocolate chips
- 2 batches flaxseed egg (14g flaxseed meal mixed into 75ml water and let it rest for 5 minutes)

Directions:
1. Heat the oven to 375 degrees F.
2. Take a muffin tray and line with cupcake liners, or simply grease with oil.
3. Add maple syrup, applesauce, baking powder, baking soda, sea salt to the flax eggs and whisk.
4. Using the whisk, add in almond milk and melted coconut oil.
5. Add all the flours and cocoa powder. Whisk it together to create a batter.
6. The batter should have a scoopable consistency.
7. Fill the muffin tray with the batter.
8. Baking for 20-28 minutes until a toothpick inserted in the center comes out clean.

9. Let them cool and put on a cooling rack later.
10. Enjoy them with any plant-based milk.

Nutrition:
Calories: 232
Carbohydrates: 31.4 g
Fiber: 3.5 g
Sugar: 16 g
Protein: 3.7 g
Fat: 11.7 g
Saturated Fat: 7.4 g
Cholesterol: 0 mg
Sodium: 249 mg

15. Simple Avocado Toast
Preparation Time: 2 minutes
Cooking Time: 5 minutes
Servings: 2
Ingredients:
- 1 slice whole grain bread
- ¼ medium avocado
- 1 pinch sea salt
- 2 teaspoons bagel seasoning (you can make your own as well)

Directions:
1. Toast the slice of bread in a toaster.
2. Mash the avocado and spread it on the toast.
3. Sprinkle it with the seasoning and sea salt.
4. Serve with plant-based milk of your choice.

Nutrition:
Calories 172
Protein 5.4g
Carbohydrates 17.8g
Fiber 5.9g
Sugars 2.3g
Fat 9.8g
Saturated fat 1.4g
Calcium 60.5mg
Magnesium 41.4mg
Potassium 341.5mg
Sodium 251.8mg

16. Aquafaba French Toast
Preparation Time: 5 minutes
Cooking Time: 10 minutes
Servings 8
Ingredients:
- ½ cup almond flour
- 1 ½ cups unsweetened & unflavored plant-based milk
- ½ teaspoon ground cinnamon
- 1 cup aquafaba
- 2 tablespoons and 1 teaspoon pure maple syrup
- 2 pinches sea salt (optional)
- ½ tablespoon orange zest
- 8 whole-grain bread (1-inch thick) slices
- ½ cup applesauce
- 1 cup fresh, frozen & thawed blueberries or raspberries

Directions:
1. Start by preheating the oven to 400 Fahrenheit and placing a wire rack on top of a baking sheet.
2. Add maple syrup, cinnamon, milk, aquafaba, flour and sea salt to a bowl and mix until smooth.
3. Add the orange zest as well.
4. Heat a pan or skillet over medium heat.
5. Dip the bread slices in the mixture, making sure they're properly coated on each side.
6. Cook the bread in the pan for 2-3 minutes or until golden brown. Make sure both sides are cooked.
7. Put the cooked toast on the wire rack and bake it in the oven for 10 minutes to make it crispy.
8. Create a chunky sauce by blending berries, applesauce and maple syrup in a blender.
9. Serve it with hot toast and enjoy!

Nutrition:
Calories 365
Fat 9.6g
Saturated Fat 6.1g
Cholesterol 0 mg
Sodium 590.1mg

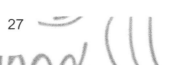

Carbohydrates 59g
Fiber 2.6g
Sugars 13g
Protein 10.6g

17. Vegan Breakfast Potatoes

Preparation Time: 10 minutes
Cooking Time: 35 minutes
Servings: 1

Ingredients:

- 1 tablespoon extra-virgin olive oil
- 1 teaspoon garlic powder
- 1 lbs. Potatoes, washed, dried and cut
- ½ teaspoon sea salt or as needed
- Fresh cracked pepper as needed
- ½ teaspoon paprika

Directions:

1. Put the oven to preheat to 425 degrees Fahrenheit and line a baking sheet with butter paper.
2. Put ½ inch cut cubed potatoes in the middle of the baking sheet and put olive oil, paprika, sea salt, garlic powder and pepper.
3. Make sure to properly mix the potatoes and spread them on the baking sheet.
4. Place them in the oven for 25 minutes.
5. Give them a toss again and bake again for 10 minutes or until the edges are golden-brown.
6. Serve hot and enjoy!

Nutrition:

Calories 127
Total Fat 2.5g
Saturated Fat 0.4g
Cholesterol 0mg
Sodium 218.4mg
Carbohydrates 24.2g
Fiber 3.7g
Sugars 1.8g
Protein 2.7g

18. Vegan Whole Wheat Waffles

Preparation Time: 5 minutes
Cooking Time: 10 minutes
Servings:

Ingredients:

- 2 tablespoons coconut sugar
- 2 cups gluten-free flour blend
- 1 tablespoon baking powder
- ¼ cup extra-virgin olive oil
- Pinch of sea salt
- 1 ¾ cups of unsweetened vanilla almond milk

Directions:

1. Read the heating instructions of your waffle maker and heat accordingly.
2. Add flour, baking powder, olive oil, sugar, and milk to a bowl.
3. Mix until no lumps remain
4. If you are not using a non-stick waffle maker, spray on some oil first.
5. Scoop up batter and pour in the center of the waffle plate
6. Shut the lid and cook following the manufacturer's instructions.
7. Open the lid once it's done and place them over a wire tray with the help of a bamboo stick or wooden spoon.
8. Serve hot with any plant-based milk or fruits.

Nutrition:

Calories 277
Fat 10.6g
Saturated Fat 1.4g
Cholesterol 0 mg
Sodium 73.7mg
Carbohydrates 44.1g
Fiber 5.3g
Sugars 5.2g
Protein 6.9g

19. Healthy Cinnamon Apples

Preparation Time: 10 minutes
Cooking Time: 10 minutes
Servings: 4

Ingredients:

- 1 tablespoon coconut oil
- 1 teaspoon vanilla extract
- 4 large peeled, cored, and ¼ inch sliced apples
- 1 teaspoon cinnamon
- 1 teaspoon cornstarch
- ½ cup cold water

- 3 tablespoons brown organic sugar

Directions:
1. Sauté the apples in a pan over medium heat for 6 minutes. Make sure to heat the oil first.
2. Make a cornstarch mixture by mixing cornstarch in water. Leave it to rest.
3. Add cinnamon, sugar, vanilla and cornstarch mixture to the apples, and stir well.
4. Keep on stirring until it starts simmering and the apples become tender.
5. Let it cool before serving with yogurt or oatmeal.

Nutrition:
Calories 126
Saturated Fat 1.9g
Cholesterol 0 mg
Sodium 6.1 mg
Carbohydrates 27.3g
Fiber 3.8g
Sugars 21.5g
Protein 0.4g

20. Vegan Chickpea Frittatas
Preparation Time: 10 minutes
Cooking Time: 35 minutes
Servings:

Ingredients:
- 1 teaspoon baking powder
- 1 teaspoon garlic powder
- 1 teaspoon dried basil
- 1 ¾ cups chickpea flour
- ¾ teaspoon sea salt
- 1 cup fresh or frozen corn
- 2 cups water
- 1 large diced red bell pepper
- 1 finely diced jalapeno
- ¼ diced spring onion
- Bunch of chopped baby kale or spinach

Directions:
1. Heat oven to 375 degrees F. Lightly grease a muffin tin if using a non-stick tin or use muffin liners if using a non-stick one.
2. Combine the chickpea flour, baking powder, salt, garlic powder, and basil in a large mixing bowl.
3. Stir in the water and add all the vegetables to the mixture.
4. Fill all 12 holes in the muffin tin with the batter using a measuring cup.
5. Place on the center rack of the oven and bake for 35 - 45 minutes
6. You can check if frittatas are ready by sticking a toothpick into the center of a muffin. If they seem soggy after 35 minutes, let them cool, and they will stiffen up.
7. Remove frittatas from the oven and turn them out onto a cooling rack to cool.
8. Serve with extra vegetables or eat as it is.

Nutrition:
Calories 150
Saturated Fat 0.3g
Cholesterol 0mg
Carbohydrates 24.1g
Fiber 4.9g
Sugars 6.1g
Protein 8.7g
Sodium 318.5mg

21. Vegetable Panini For Breakfast
Preparation Time: 5 minutes
Cooking Time: 10 minutes
Servings: 1

Ingredients:
- ¼ cup raisins
- 2 slices of whole wheat bread
- ¼ cup hot water
- ¼ cup organic peanut butter
- 1 tablespoon cinnamon
- 2 teaspoons cacao powder
- 1 ripe banana

Directions:
1. Combine cacao powder, raisins, cinnamon and hot water in a bowl.
2. Take bread slices and apply peanut butter on them.
3. Slice the bananas and layer them on top of the bread.

4. Blend the raisins mixture in the blender until smooth.
5. Spread the mixture onto the banana, peanut butter toast.
6. Serve it immediately.

Nutrition:
Calories: 850
Fats 34 g
Carbohydrates 112 g
Proteins 27

22. Sweet Potatoes Breakfast Smoothie
Preparation Time: 5 minutes
Cooking Time: 10 minutes
Servings: 1
Ingredients:
- 1 ½ cups unsweetened almond milk
- ½ frozen banana
- ½ cup frozen zucchini pieces
- ½ teaspoon sea salt
- 1 cup cooked and cubed frozen sweet potato
- ¼ cup nutmeg
- 1 scoop vanilla protein powder
- 1 tablespoon almond butter

Directions:
1. Add all the ingredients mentioned above in the blender.
2. Blend the ingredients on high speed for 2-3 minutes, or until everything's smooth.
3. Pour the smoothie into a glass and enjoy your super-healthy breakfast.

Nutrition:
Calories: 235
Fat: 9.2 g
Carbs: 24 g
Protein: 14.6 g
Fiber: 2.4

23. Quinoa & Breakfast Patties
Preparation Time: 3 minutes
Cooking Time: 6 minutes
Servings: 4
Ingredients:
- 2 flax eggs (water and flaxseed meal)
- 1 cup cooked quinoa
- ½ cup shredded carrots
- 2 teaspoons parsley
- ½ cup shredded broccoli florets
- 1 ½ teaspoon garlic powder
- 1 ½ teaspoon onion powder
- ¼ teaspoon black pepper
- ⅓ teaspoon salt
- 2 cloves of minced garlic
- 2 tablespoons coconut oil
- ½ gluten-free bread crumbs

Directions:
1. Leaving oil, add all the ingredients to a large bowl and stir well.
2. Turn the mixture into patties.
3. Place a skillet pan over medium heat and heat oil.
4. Once hot, place your shaped patties and cool for 2-3 minutes each side until golden-brown.
5. Serve immediately with your favorite sides.

Nutrition:
Calories: 229.6
Fat: 11.1 g
Carbs: 27.7g
Protein: 9.3g
Fiber: 6.6 g

24. Chia Seed Vanilla Overnight Pudding
Preparation Time: 4 hours
Cooking Time: 4 hours
Servings: 4
Ingredients:
- ½ cup chia seeds
- 2 cups unsweetened almond milk (or any plant-based milk)
- 1 tablespoon maple syrup or as needed
- 2 teaspoons vanilla essence or real extract

Directions:
1. Mix all the ingredients in a bowl
2. Leave the mixture for 5 minutes, and return to give a mix a second time.
3. When properly mixed, cover the bowl and refrigerate for 4 hours or overnight.

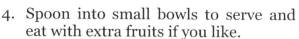

4. Spoon into small bowls to serve and eat with extra fruits if you like.

Nutrition:
Calories 165
Saturated Fat 0.9g
Cholesterol 0 mg
Sodium 98 mg
Carbohydrates 15.3g
Fiber 8.9g
Sugars 3.3g
Protein 5.1g

25. Healthy Smoothie Bowl
Preparation Time: 10 minutes
Cooking Time: 10 minutes
Servings: 2
Ingredients:
- 2 fresh and frozen bananas
- 2 tablespoons almond butter or any nut butter
- ½ - ¾ cup unsweetened plant-based milk
- 1 ½ cups frozen fruit mix
- Granola (optional)
- Fresh fruits (optional)

Directions:
1. Blend all the ingredients in a blender except optional products until smooth and thick.
2. Take out the mixture into a bowl.
3. Serve topped with fruits or granola.

Nutrition:
Calories 212
Saturated Fat 0.8g
Cholesterol 0 mg
Sodium 3.1 mg
Carbohydrate 31.5g
Fiber 6.1g
Sugars 16.8g
Protein 5g

26. Colorful Broiled Grapefruit Breakfast
Preparation Time: 5 minutes
Cooking Time: 10 minutes
Servings: 2
Ingredients:
- 2 tablespoons brown sugar

- 2 teaspoons pure maple syrup
- 1 teaspoon ground ginger
- Sea salt to taste
- Pinch of cinnamon
- 2 sliced in half grapefruits

Directions:
1. Preheat a broiler or the oven to a high temperature.
2. Take half sliced grapefruit and make sure they stand straight.
3. To cut each segment, use a paring knife to separate the pink flesh from the membrane.
4. After, gently remove the rind by paring around the entire outside of the fruit. It will make grapefruit eating a little smoother and easier.
5. Place each half, the flesh facing upwards, on a rimmed baking sheet.
6. Top each half with 1 teaspoon or so of maple syrup, 1 teaspoon brown sugar, and a dash of ginger with your fingers, coating the flesh.
7. Place under the broiler or in the oven and cook for 4 – 7 minutes until the sugar is caramelized or the sides are slightly brown.
8. Let it cool at room temperature and serve with sea salt and cinnamon on top.

Nutrition:
Calories: 179
Fat 10.3g
Saturated Fat 8.4g
Cholesterol 0 mg
Sodium 0.1mg
Carbohydrates 22.6g
Fiber 2.5g
Sugars 20g
Protein 1.6g

27. Vegan Strawberry Banana Milkshake
Preparation Time: 5 minutes
Cooking Time: 5 minutes
Servings: 1
Ingredients:
- 1 frozen, peeled and cubed banana

- 1 tablespoon pure maple syrup
- 1 teaspoon vanilla extract
- 1 cup unsweetened plain almond milk
- 1 scoop protein powder
- 1 cup frozen strawberries
- Dairy-free whipped cream (optional)

Directions:
1. Add all the ingredients to a blender except the cream.
2. Blend it until smooth.
3. Serve in a glass with whipped cream on top.

Nutrition:
Calories 254
Fat 3.3g
Saturated Fat 0.1g
Cholesterol 0mg
Sodium 193.8mg
Carbohydrates 54.3g
Fiber 5.2g
Sugars 35.4g
Protein 3.1g

28. Vegetable Tofu Scramble
Preparation Time: 5 minutes
Cooking Time: 15 minutes
Servings: 4

Ingredients:
- 16 oz organic firm tofu
- 1 tablespoon extra-virgin olive oil
- ½ diced onion
- 1 cup broccoli florets
- 1 large diced tomato
- 6 oz sliced mushrooms
- ½ teaspoon garlic powder
- ½ teaspoon cumin
- Kale or spinach bunch
- ½ teaspoon turmeric
- Sea salt & pepper as needed
- 1 tablespoon nutritional yeast (skip if you are allergic)
- 1 teaspoon red pepper flakes
- Avocado for serving

Directions:
1. Place a skillet or wok on medium heat and add oil.
2. Once oil is hot, sauté onions for 4 minutes or until golden brown.
3. Drain tofu, crumble it with your hands, and add to the pan.
4. Add the rest of the vegetables and dry ingredients
5. Add nutritional yeast and mix. Wait for the greens to cook.
6. Once done, remove from heat and serve on a plate with avocados.

Nutrition:
Calories 181
Fat 9.9g
Saturated Fat 1.4g
Cholesterol 0 mg
Sodium 130mg
Carbohydrate 13.5g
Fiber 5.3g
Sugars 4.2g
Protein 15.6

Chapter 5: Vegetables

29. Potatoes & Peas Creamy Curry

Preparation Time: 15 minutes
Cooking Time: 30 minutes
Servings: 4

Ingredients:
- 8 small & diced potatoes
- 2 cups water
- 1 cup frozen peas
- 1 tablespoon extra-virgin olive oil
- 3 tablespoons tomato paste
- 1 small ¼ inch cut pieces of onion
- 3 teaspoons curry powder
- 1 teaspoon sea salt
- 1 peeled & minced fresh ginger
- A pinch of black pepper
- ⅓ cup chopped cilantro

Directions:
9. Place a large wok on medium heat and heat oil.
10. Add potatoes and cook for 10 minutes or until lightly brown.
11. Move the potatoes to one side of the pan, and add ginger, garlic and onion.
12. Cook and stir for five minutes until you can smell the aroma.
13. Then mix the potatoes with the rest and add curry powder and water to the mixture.
14. Turn on high heat and bring the water to a boil.
15. Now lower the heat and cook the potatoes while stirring until their tender.
16. Add in the peas, salt, and tomatoes until the curry turns into a creamy gravy.
17. Season with pepper and salt as you like and serve with fresh cilantro.

Nutrition:
Calories: 323
Fat: 4g
Carbohydrates: 65g
Protein: 9g
Fiber: 9g

Sodium:654mg

30. Plant-Based Vegetable Wrap

Preparation Time: 5 minutes
Cooking Time: 10 minutes
Servings: 1
Ingredients:
- 2 tablespoons fresh lemon juice,
- ¼ cup Hummus
- 2 Romaine lettuce leaves
- ½ cup cherry tomatoes
- 2 tablespoons quartered Kalamata olives
- A bunch of baby spinach
- ¼ cup cooked chickpeas

Directions:
7. Combine everything except hummus and lettuce.
8. Spread hummus on the lettuce wraps and add the mixture.
9. Roll the lettuce wraps and serve.

Nutrition:
Calories: 428
Protein: 13 g
Fats: 23 g
Carbohydrates: 47 g

31. Vegan Spinach Ricotta

Preparation Time: 15 minutes
Cooking Time: 50 minutes
Servings: 7

Ingredients:
- 20 oz frozen, thawed and drained spinach
- 4 cups pasta sauce
- 3 cups vegan ricotta
- 14 cannelloni tubes

Directions:
1. Turn the oven on to 350 degrees Fahrenheit.
2. Combine the spinach and ricotta.
3. In a baking dish, pour 2 cups of pasta sauce.

4. Fill cannelloni tubes with a piping bag filled with spinach and ricotta mixture.
5. Arrange the filled tubes in the baking dish and add the rest of the sauce.
6. Bake for 40 minutes, covered.
7. Remove the cover and bake for 5 to 10 minutes more.
8. Allow to cool for a few minutes before serving.

Nutrition:
Calories 473
Fat 28.5g
Saturated Fat 4.3g
Cholesterol 0 mg
Sodium 384.9mg
Carbohydrates 43g
Fibers 6.3g
Sugars 8.1g
Protein 16.9g

32. Vegan Asparagus Lasagna
Preparation Time: 10 minutes
Cooking Time: 30 minutes
Servings: 2
Ingredients:
- 1 lb. Ends trimmed asparagus
- 1 cup cooked, drained, and rinsed lentils
- 12 whole-grain lasagna noodles
- 2 cups vegan ricotta
- 1 jar pasta sauce
- Extra-virgin olive oil
- Sea salt as needed

Directions:
4. Turn your oven to 400 degrees.
5. Cook your lasagna noodles and leave to rest.
6. Take a baking dish and add half pasta sauce, layer three noodles, half ricotta cheese, half lentils, and repeat.
7. Layer the top with asparagus coated in a little olive oil and sea salt.
8. Bake for 20 minutes or until asparagus turn tender.
9. Serve after letting it cool first.

Nutrition:
Calories 422

Fat 1.2
Saturated Fat 0.2g
Cholesterol 0 mg
Sodium 248.8mg
Carbohydrates 84.4g
Fiber 8.5g
Sugars 0.4g
Protein 17.2g

33. Simple Scalloped Potatoes
Preparation Time: 15 minutes
Cooking Time: 55 minutes
Servings: 4
Ingredients:
- 4 minced garlic cloves
- 2 ½ tablespoons extra-virgin olive oil
- ½ cup vegetable broth
- 4 tablespoons nutritional yeast
- ¼ vegan parmesan cheese
- ¼ teaspoon sea salt
- Black pepper as needed
- ⅛ teaspoon nutmeg
- ⅓ medium sliced potatoes
- 1 ½ cups unsweetened plain almond milk
- 2 ½ tablespoons cornstarch
- ¼ teaspoon paprika
- Fresh parsley

Directions:
9. Turn on oven to 350 degrees Fahrenheit and heat a 10-inch over-safe skillet over medium heat.
10. Add in olive oil, salt, garlic and pepper and sauté until slightly golden brown.
11. Whisk in cornstarch and cook for a minute.
12. Whisk in almond milk slowly to avoid clumps.
13. Then whisk in the vegetable broth and reduce heat to a simmer.
14. Let the liquid thicken while stirring occasionally.
15. Remove skillet from stove and transfer the sauce to a blender.
16. Add in a dash of sea salt, black pepper, nutmeg and nutritional yeast, and blend on high setting until smooth.

17. Check to taste and adjust the seasonings as needed.
18. Reuse the skillet after washing and drying and lightly grease with oil.
19. Spread half of the potatoes in the dish and season with salt and pepper.
20. Make sure they're properly coated and then add cheese.
21. Add the rest of the potatoes, repeat the seasoning, and cover the potatoes with the sauce in the blender.
22. The potatoes should lie below the sauce. If any slice is above the surface, remove it.
23. Cover with foil and bake for 20 minutes in the oven.
24. Next remove the foil and bake for 40 minutes more.
25. Potatoes should be knife-tender when done.
26. Remove from oven and allow it to cool before serving with parsley and paprika.

Nutrition:
Calories: 238
Carbohydrates: 24.8 g
Protein: 8.5 g
Fat: 12.5 g
Saturated Fat: 1.6 g
Sodium: 342 mg
Potassium: 613 mg
Fiber: 3.8 g
Sugar: 1.1 g

34. Vegan Zucchini Wraps With Kale Pesto
Preparation Time: 10 minutes
Cooking Time: 30 minutes
Servings: 2
Ingredients:
- Cilantro
- Toothpicks
- 1 julienned red bell pepper
- 1 julienned yellow bell pepper
- Quartered baby carrots
- Basil leaves
- 2 long thinly sliced zucchini
- Fresh cracked pepper
- Sea salt as needed
- 2 tablespoons almonds
- 2 tablespoons tahini
- 2 cups kale
- 1 clove garlic
- 3 tablespoons extra-virgin olive oil

Directions:
11. Add kale, garlic, olive oil, sea salt, almonds and tahini to a blender or food processor until smooth yet thick. Check for taste and adjust the salt.
12. Place zucchini strips flat on the surface, apply the pesto sauce in the processor, put fresh basil, red, yellow bell pepper and baby carrots one of each onto the strip.
13. Make sure you leave enough space for wrapping.
14. Roll the stripe in a wrap and stick a toothpick in the center to hold everything.
15. Season with cilantro, sea salt and cracked pepper. Serve immediately!

Nutrition:
Calories: 47
Fat 1.9g
Saturated Fat 0.3g
Cholesterol 0 mg
Sodium 52 mg
Carbohydrate 6.8g
Fiber 1.9g
Sugars 2.9g
Protein 1.8g

35. Creamy Turnip Mash
Preparation Time: 20 minutes
Cooking Time: 35 Minutes
Servings: 4
Ingredients:
- 4 tablespoons vegan butter
- 2 cups water
- 1 cup oat milk
- 1 ½ lbs. peeled, boiled and cut into small pieces turnips
- 1 tablespoon chopped fresh parsley
- 2 fresh chopped rosemary sprigs
- 1 teaspoon ginger garlic paste (or make your own)

- 1 teaspoon red chili flakes
- Sea salt & black pepper as needed

Directions:
5. Boil turnips in water for 30 minutes and drain once done.
6. Add parsley, vegan butter, milk, rosemary, red chili pepper, salt, ginger garlic paste to turnips.
7. Blend everything with a hand blender.
8. Serve with a dash of black pepper and salt if needed.

Nutrition:
Calories: 187
Fat: 13.6g
Carbohydrates: 14g
Protein: 3.6g

36. Vegan Beetroot Hummus
Preparation Time: 35 minutes
Cooking Time: 60 Minutes
Servings: 4
Ingredients:
- 3 small beetroots
- 1 teaspoon sea salt
- 1 teaspoon minced garlic
- ½ teaspoon paprika
- ¼ red chili pepper flakes
- 1 fresh lemon juice
- 2 tablespoons extra-virgin olive oil
- 2 tablespoons tahini
- 15 oz. cooked chickpeas
- 1 tablespoon chopped cilantro
- 1 tablespoon chopped almonds

Directions:
10. Turn on the oven to 425 degrees.
11. Coat beets with oil and sprinkle salt.
12. Wrap the beets in foil from top and place in the oven for an hour.
13. Once done, allow it to cool.
14. When It is cool enough, remove the skin and cut them small enough to fit in a food processor.
15. Add the rest of the ingredients and process until smooth.
16. Transfer the hummus to a bowl and serve with whole-grain bread or enjoy with cucumbers.

Nutrition:
Calories: 50.1
Fat: 2.5 g
Carbohydrates: 5 g
Protein: 2 g
Fiber: 1 g

37. Healthy Zucchanoush
Preparation Time: 5 minutes
Cooking Time: 10 Minutes
Servings: 7
Ingredients:
- 1 tablespoon toasted pine nuts
- 1 lbs. quartered in length small zucchini
- ⅔ tablespoons sea salt
- ½ teaspoon minced garlic
- 3 tablespoon mint leaves
- 2 tablespoons fresh lemon juice
- ⅓ teaspoon ground black pepper
- 3 tablespoons extra-virgin olive oil

Directions:
7. Transfer zucchini to a bowl, put in oil, sea salt, and toss to combine.
8. Grill it for 10 minutes on medium heat until crispy on all sides.
9. Add grilled zucchini to a blender with the remaining ingredients, leaving nuts and mint.
10. Blend until smooth and transfer the sauce to a bowl.
11. Garnish with nuts and mint and enjoy!

Nutrition:
Calories: 125
Fat: 11.5 g
Carbs: 4.5 g
Protein: 3 g
Fiber: 1 g

38. Nutritious Mashed Root Vegetables
Preparation Time: 10 minutes
Cooking Time: 25 Minutes
Servings: 5
Ingredients:
- ½ pound trimmed and diced carrots
- 1lbs. peeled russet potatoes chunks

- 4 tablespoons vegan butter
- ½ teaspoon dried dill weed
- 1 teaspoon dried basil
- 1 teaspoon oregano
- ½ teaspoon dried marjoram
- ½ pound trimmed & diced parnips
- Water as needed

Directions:
9. Boil the vegetables for 25 minutes until tender.
10. Drain the remaining water.
11. Add the rest of the herbs and ingredients, except water and mash with a masher or hand blender.
12. Once smooth and liquid, dish out in a bowl and serve immediately.

Nutrition:
Calories: 207
Fat: 9.5g
Carbs: 29.1g
Protein 3g

39. Vegan Super food Bowl
Preparation Time: 10 minutes
Cooking Time: 15 minutes
Servings: 4
Ingredients:
- 8 oz. microwavable quinoa pouch
- 2 tablespoons fresh lemon juice
- 8 oz. cooked & sliced whole baby beets
- ½ cup hummus
- 5 oz. baby kale
- 1 medium sliced avocado
- 1 cup frozen shelled & thawed edamame
- ¼ cup unsalted toasted sunflower seeds
- Water as needed

Directions:
6. Follow the cooking instructions on the quinoa package. Let aside to cool.
7. Add hummus and lemon juice in a small bowl, and use water if needed to adjust the dressing consistency.
8. Divide the dressing into 4 small food containers with covers and put in the refrigerator.

9. Divide baby kale among those 4 container bowls,
10. Next, put quinoa, half cup beets, ¼ cup edamame and 1 tablespoon sunflower seeds.
11. Serve with avocado and hummus dressing whenever you are ready to eat.

Nutrition:
Calories 381
Protein 16.2g
Carbohydrates 43.1g
Fiber 13.2g
Sugars 7.7g
Fat 18.6g
Saturated fat 2.4g
Potassium 1065.8mg
Sodium 188.2 mg

40. Grilled Mixed Vegetables
Preparation Time: 9 minutes
Cooking Time: 16 minutes
Servings: 4
Ingredients:
- 1 zucchini
- 8 oz. stemmed cremini mushrooms
- 1 red bell pepper
- 1 small red onion
- 1 yellow squash
- 1 green bell pepper
- 1 ear 1-inch thick cut rounds of fresh corn
- Sea salt as needed
- Extra-virgin olive oil as needed
- Freshly ground pepper as needed

Directions:
9. Set the griller to medium heat, spray or apply cooking oil to the grill plate.
10. Cut the vegetables into thick slices. Size should be the same and pierce into metal skewers much like a chicken shashlik.
11. Drizzle oil and season with salt and pepper
12. Grill the skewered vegetables each side until tender & slightly charred.

13. Once done, take off from the grill, season as needed and serve with a dressing of your liking.

Nutrition:
Calories 77
Fat 4.6g
Saturated Fat 0.7g
Trans Fat 0g
Cholesterol 0 mg
Sodium 67mg
Potassium 398mg
Carbohydrates 8.7g
Fiber 2.7g
Sugars 4.6g
Protein 2.4g

41. Nutritious Tofu & Asparagus Stir Fry

Preparation Time: 10 minutes
Cooking Time: 20 minutes
Servings: 3

Ingredients:
- 8 oz. chopped in slices firm tofu
- 2 tablespoons hoisin sauce
- 4 thinly sliced spring onions
- 1 tablespoon peeled & minced ginger
- 1 bunch of trimmed & chopped asparagus
- 1 handful fresh & chopped mint
- 1 handful fresh & chopped basil
- 1 handful chopped & toasted cashew nuts
- 3 cloves chopped garlic
- 1 fresh lemon juice & zest
- Toasted sesame oil as needed
- 3 handfuls chopped spinach
- Sea salt as needed
- Red chili flakes as needed

Directions:
7. Take a pan or wok and heat up oil on medium heat.
8. Cook the tofu for a few minutes and then move it to the side of the wok.
9. Sauté in red chili flakes, onions, ginger, salt and asparagus, stir for one minute.

10. Next, throw in garlic, cashews and spinach. Stir and cook for two minutes.
11. Mix the tofu with the rest of the ingredients in the wok and drizzle fresh lemon juice.
12. Zest and hoisin sauce. Cook for half a minute.
13. Remove the pan from the heat and serve with mint and basil.

Nutrition:
Calories 300
Fat 20g
Saturated Fat 35g
Cholesterol 0 mg
Sodium 440mg
Potassium 630 mg
Carbohydrates 26g
Fiber 5g
Sugars 8g
Protein 9g

42. Yummy Kale Chips

Preparation Time: 10 minutes
Cooking Time: 10 minutes
Servings: 8

Ingredients:
- 1 tablespoon extra-virgin olive oil
- 1 bunch stemless, washed and drained Kale
- Sea salt as needed

Directions:
4. Start by preheating the oven 325 degrees Fahrenheit.
5. Transfer the cut leaves into a large bowl and massage the oil until covered.
6. Season with sea salt and toss to combine.
7. Line a baking sheet with parchment paper and place leaves on them, leaving a little gap otherwise they won't bake properly.
8. Use another baking sheet if needed.
9. Bake them for 10 minutes or until the edges turn crisp.
10. Serve with sea salt.

Nutrition:
Calories 21
Fat 2.3g
Saturated Fat 0.3g
Cholesterol 0 mg
Sodium 0.8mg
Carbohydrates 0.20
Fiber 0.1g
Sugars 0g
Protein 0.1g

43. Healthy Vegetable Chili
Preparation Time: 15 minutes
Cooking Time: 6 hours
Servings: 4
Ingredients:
- 2 peeled and cut into medium chunks sweet potatoes
- 2 teaspoons ground cumin
- 2 teaspoons smoked paprika
- 3 tablespoons extra-virgin olive oil
- 2 chopped carrots
- 1 chopped onion
- 2 crushed garlic cloves
- 2 chopped celery sticks
- 1 tablespoon tomato puree
- 1 teaspoon dried oregano
- 1 cut in chunks red pepper
- 400g can drained black beans
- 2 400g can chopped tomatoes
- 400g can drained kidney beans
- Guacamole to serve
- Coriander as needed

Directions:
6. Place a frying pan over medium heat and heat the oil.
7. Once hot, add onion, carrot and celery and cook for 8-10 until soft.
8. Make sure to stir frequently.
9. Once soft, add in crushed garlic and sweet potato chunks.
10. Cook for 1 minute, and add oregano, all the dried spices, and tomato puree.
11. Cook for 1 minute and transfer this mixture to a slow cooker.
12. Throw in red pepper and chopped tomatoes. Stir everything properly and cook for 5 hours.

13. Mix in the beans and cook for 3/ minutes more.
14. Serve with guacamole and season with coriander as needed.

Nutrition:
Calories: 367
Fat: 10g
Carbohydrates: 48g
Saturated fat: 2g
Sugars: 22g
Protein: 12g
Fiber: 17g
Salt: 0.6g

44. Vegetable Kebabs With Coconut Sauce
Preparation Time: 10 minutes
Cooking Time: 10 minutes
Servings: 4
Ingredients:
- Solid Vegetables, boiled & diced, of any choice
- 1 tablespoon extra-virgin olive oil
- 2 crushed garlic cloves
- 2 teaspoons ground cumin
- 4 green shallots
- 1 teaspoon crushed ginger
- 1 teaspoon paprika
- 1 tablespoon fresh lemon juice
- 2 tablespoons chili sauce
- Tofu squared
- 1 ½ coconut cream
- 1 ½ tablespoon finely chopped coriander
- Boiled brown rice (optional)

Direction:
5. Thread vegetables and tofu onto bamboo skewers.
6. Keep somewhere warm.
7. Blend all the ingredients except the vegetables and tofu in the blender to create a coconut cream sauce.
8. Pour the sauce on the vegetable kebabs to eat, or enjoy with brown rice.

Nutrition:
Calories: 266.75
Fat: 11.08g

Sodium: 85.95mg
Potassium: 295.24mg
Carbs: 40.79g
Sugars: 33.89g
Fiber: 2.18g
Protein: 2.87g

45. Plant-Based Style Green Beans
Preparation Time: 15 minutes
Cooking Time: 14 minutes
Servings: 4
Ingredients:
- A handful of fresh dill sprigs
- 2 lbs. Green beans
- 3 medium sized onions divided
- 14 oz. Can diced tomatoes
- 3 cloves of minced garlic
- ¼ cup clean water
- 4 teaspoons black pepper
- 3 tablespoons extra-virgin olive oil
- 3 teaspoons granulated pure cane sugar
- 2 tablespoons tomato paste
- ¾ 2 teaspoons sea salt
- 1 cup of coconut cream
- 2 tablespoons lemon juice

Directions:
4. Cut the green beans into ½ inch pieces, wash, drain and set aside.
5. Cut two onions and peel the skin of the third one, but leave it whole.
6. Place a heavy-bottomed pan over medium heat and heat oil.
7. Stir in the cut onions and cook until translucent.
8. Add in tomato paste, diced tomatoes, sugar, black pepper, sea salt, and water.
9. Stir in green beans and combine everything.
10. Place the whole onion in the pan and cover.
11. Let the water come to a boil and turn the heat to low-medium.
12. Cook until the beans are tender and stir occasionally.

13. Take a bowl and add coconut cream, garlic, lemon juice, and ¾ teaspoon sea salt.
14. Whisk it and adjust the seasoning if needed.
15. Serve the green beans on a plate with coconut sauce on top and fresh dill.

Nutrition:
Calories: 283
Carbohydrates: 38g
Protein: 9g
Fat: 13g
Saturated Fat: 3g
Cholesterol: 8mg
Sodium: 1848 mg
Potassium: 1055mg
Fiber: 9g
Sugar: 22g

46. Perfect Mashed Potatoes
Preparation Time: 10 minutes
Cooking Time: 30 minutes
Servings: 4
Ingredients:
- 3-4 tablespoons softened plant-based butter
- ¼ cup fresh chives
- 5 roasted minced garlic cloves
- 6-8 medium sized potatoes
- 1 ½ teaspoon sea salt
- ½ teaspoon ground black pepper
- Water

Directions:
9. Peel the potatoes, cut them in halves and put them in water in a large pot.
10. Bring it to a boil over high heat and put in 1 teaspoon of salt.
11. Cook for 25 minutes or so until knife-tender.
12. Drain potatoes and set aside for 1 minute to cool.
13. Use a potato masher to mash them until fluffy.
14. Add in garlic, ½ teaspoon salt, butter and black pepper and mix to combine.
15. Test the taste to adjust the seasoning.
16. Chop up the chives and serve them on top of the mashed potatoes.

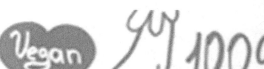

Nutrition:
Calories: 247
Carbohydrates: 40.5 g
Protein: 4.9 g
Fat: 8.3 g
Saturated Fat: 2.3 g
Cholesterol: 0 mg
Sodium: 956 mg
Potassium: 958 mg
Fiber: 3.2 g
Sugar: 1.6 g

47. Flavorful Black Bean Avocado Tacos

Preparation Time: 10 minutes
Cooking Time: 20 minutes
Servings: 10

Ingredients:

- ½ cup vegetable stock or water
- ¼ cup for water
- 15oz. Drained and rinsed black beans
- 1 small seeded and diced jalapeno
- ½ teaspoon garlic powder
- ½ teaspoon dried oregano
- 1 teaspoon cumin
- Sea salt
- Sliced avocado
- Warm corn tortillas
- Shredded lettuce
- Chopped Cilantro
- Corn salsa

Directions:

4. Sauté onions in warm oil in a pot over medium heat. Give it 5 minutes or until golden-brown.
5. Combine all the powder ingredients and jalapeno and cook for 1 minute until you smell a nice aroma.
6. Add beans and ¼ cup water, put the lid on and reduce heat to a simmer for 5 minutes.
7. Remove the pan from heat and use a silicone spatula to mash ½ of the beans.
8. Add more water as needed for your desired consistency.

9. Take your tortillas and warm both sides until slightly crispy over a pan on a low-medium flame.
10. Lay a tortilla flat on a hard surface, put ½ cup of beans, chopped cilantro, shredded lettuce and sliced avocado. Season with salt and serve immediately.

Nutrition:
Calories 463
Fat 6.6g
Saturated Fat 1g
Cholesterol 0 mg
Sodium 739.8mg
Carbohydrates 90.8g
Fiber 20.5g
Sugars 5.4g
Protein 16g

48. Vegetable One Pot Orzo

Preparation Time: 10 minutes
Cooking Time: 25 minutes
Servings: 6

Ingredients:

- 15.5oz. can drained & rinsed black beans
- 10oz. can diced tomatoes
- 2 tablespoons extra-virgin olive oil
- 1 diced red bell pepper
- 1 diced green bell pepper
- 3 minced garlic cloves
- 1 diced yellow onion
- 2 teaspoons ground cumin
- 1 teaspoon chili powder
- Sea salt as needed
- Black pepper as needed
- Green chilies
- 1 ½ cups frozen corn
- 3 ½ cups vegetable broth
- 16oz. orzo pasta

Directions:

- Add olive oil to a large pot over medium high heat and heat until glossy.
- Sauté in onion, garlic, red and green bell pepper for 5 minutes or until soft and fragrant.

- Stir in cumin, chili powder, salt, and pepper until combined.
- Stir in black beans, diced tomatoes, green chilies, corn, and orzo.
- Gradually pour the vegetable stock and bring it to a boil
- Turn the heat to low-medium, put the lid on and let simmer until the pasta is cooked and the liquid has vanished.
- Give it 13 minutes and stir occasionally.
- Serve hot and enjoy!

Nutrition:
Calories: 477
Carbohydrates: 83g
Protein: 19g
Fat: 9g
Fiber: 9g
Sugar: 11g

Chapter 6: Soup & Stews

49. Flavorful Chickpea Noodle Soup

Preparation Time: 10 minutes
Cooking Time: 20 minutes
Servings: 4

Ingredients:

- 3 large peeled & diced carrots
- 2 cans drained and rinsed chickpeas
- 10 cups vegetable broth or water
- 12 oz. Whole wheat pasta
- 1 diced onion
- 1 tablespoon extra-virgin olive oil
- ¼ cup fresh chopped parsley
- 1 teaspoon dried thyme
- 1 teaspoon dried oregano
- 1 teaspoon dried basil
- 3 ribs sliced celery
- Sea salt as needed
- Black pepper as needed
- Lemon wedges

Directions:

1. Warm oil, then cook onion, celery, carrots, and herbs for 6 minutes in a large pan over medium heat.
2. Stir in the chickpeas, liquids and paste to the pan.
3. Bring to a boil and let it simmer for 7 minutes on low heat or until the paste is tender.
4. Lastly, add in parsley and sprinkle salt and pepper as needed.
5. Serve in a bowl with lemon wedges!

Nutrition:

Calories: 362
Fat: 3.1g
Saturated Fat: 0.4g
Cholesterol: 0mg
Sodium: 411.2mg
Carbohydrates: 69.5g
Fiber: 9g
Sugars: 8.5g
Protein: 14.4g

50. Creamy Vegetable Miso Soup

Preparation Time: 15 minutes
Cooking Time: 15 minutes
Servings: 4

Ingredients:

- 4 cups of water
- ½ medium peeled, seeded & cut into small pieces butternut squash
- 1 bunch stemmed and leaves chopped small kale
- 1 ½ teaspoons sea salt
- 1 ½ teaspoons onion powder
- 2 each 15 oz. Cannellini beans drained & rinsed cans
- ½ teaspoon smoked paprika
- 1 teaspoon red miso paste
- Red chili flakes

Directions:

1. Take a medium saucepan, add squash and 2 cups of water.
2. Bring it to a boil over high heat.
3. Set the heat to medium and cook until tender.
4. Use a second silicone spatula and add half of the tender squash to a blender.
5. Add the rest of the water and blend until smooth.
6. Transfer the blended squash back to the pot.
7. Put in cannellini beans, sea salt, kale, onion, garlic powder and smoked paprika.
8. Bring to a boil and cook for 5 minutes or until the kale is softened.
9. Take off the heat, add miso and stir until the miso gets absorbed.
10. Serve into bowls and season with red chili flakes.

Nutrition:

Calories: 273
Fat: 2g
Carbohydrates 53g
Protein: 16g
Fiber: 19g

Sodium: 961 mg

51. Healthy Tomato Barley Soup
Preparation Time: 20 minutes
Cooking Time: 40 minutes
Servings: 6
Ingredients:
- 2 ½ cups of water
- 2 tablespoons extra-virgin olive oil
- 10.75 oz. vegetable broth
- ¼ cup barley
- 14.5 oz. Peeled & diced potatoes
- 1 cup chopped celery
- 2 diced tomatoes
- 1 cup chopped onions
- 1 cup chopped carrots
- 2 teaspoons minced garlic
- 1 teaspoon sea salt
- ⅛ teaspoon ground black pepper

Directions:
1. Place a large sauce pan over medium heat and heat oil.
2. Sauté in onions, garlic, carrots and celery. Cook until tender.
3. Add the rest of the ingredients and bring the soup to a boil.
4. Bring the heat to a simmer and let it be for 40 minutes.
5. Serve immediately!

Nutrition:
Calories: 129
Fat: 5.5 g
Carbohydrates: 15.3 g
Protein: 4.6 g
Fiber: 3.7g

52. Vegan Carrot Coriander Soup
Preparation Time: 10 minutes
Cooking Time: 20 minutes
Servings: 4
Ingredients:
- 14 oz. chickpeas
- 2 tablespoons extra-virgin olive oil
- ½ large yellow onion
- 1lb. Peeled & sliced carrots
- 5 cups low-sodium vegetable broth
- ¼ cup chopped cilantro
- ½ teaspoon turmeric

- ½ teaspoon cumin
- A pinch of sea salt and as needed
- 1 large peeled & cubed sweet potato
- 1 teaspoon coriander
- Fresh cracked pepper as needed

Directions:
1. Start by preheating the oven to 400 degrees Fahrenheit.
2. Line a baking sheet with parchment paper or grease with oil.
3. Drain, rinse, and dry chickpeas.
4. Combine chickpeas, cumin, salt, oil, turmeric and toss to mix well.
5. Transfer the mixture to the baking tray in a single spread.
6. Bake for 45 minutes and mix one. Allow it to cool once done.
7. Heat oil in a large pot over medium heat.
8. Sauté in onions for 5 minutes, and combine sweet potato, carrots and coriander, and stir for a minute.
9. Add broth and bring to a boil, then let it simmer for 20 minutes on low heat or until softened.
10. Remove from stove and allow it to cool.
11. Use a hand blender to puree the soup and use extra water if needed to adjust the consistency.
12. Serve in a bowl with roasted chickpeas and cilantro on top.

Nutrition:
Calories: 342
Fat: 17.9g
Saturated Fat: 13.4g
Cholesterol: 5mg
Sodium: 1924.4mg
Carbohydrates: 39.7g
Fiber: 11.2g
Sugars: 10.7g
Protein: 10.5g

53. Italian Cremini Mushroom Soup
Preparation Time: 10 minutes
Cooking Time: 15 Minutes
Servings: 3

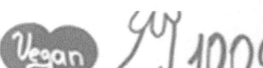

Ingredients:

- 3 cups water
- 3 cups chopped cremini mushrooms
- 3 tablespoons vegan butter
- 2 tablespoons almond flour
- 1 chopped red bell pepper
- 1 chopped onion
- ½ teaspoon minced garlic
- 1 teaspoon Italian herb mix
- Sea salt as needed
- Black pepper as needed
- 1 tablespoon chopped fresh chives

Directions:

1. Place a pot over medium heat and melt the butter.
2. Sauté in onion and pepper for three minutes until translucent.
3. Stir in cremini mushrooms and garlic and cook until tender.
4. Sprinkle almond flour over the mushrooms and cook for a minute.
5. Add the rest of the ingredients.
6. Let the water simmer until it thickens.
7. Serve in soup bowls with fresh chives.

Nutrition:

Calories: 154
Fat: 12.3g
Carbohydrates: 9.6g
Protein: 4.4g

54. Thai Squash Soup

Preparation Time: 10 minutes
Cooking Time: 30 Minutes
Servings: 2

Ingredients:

- 13.5oz coconut milk can
- 1 tablespoon extra-virgin olive oil
- 1 chunked butternut squash
- 1 chopped onion
- 1 pint vegetable stock
- 1 teaspoon curry powder

Directions:

1. Place a pan on the stove and heat oil.
2. Add chopped onion and stir for 2 minutes or until tender.
3. Stir in butternut squash, stock and curry powder

4. Bring to a boil and lower heat to a simmer.
5. Once the squash is tender, mix in the coconut.
6. Add it all to a blender and blend until smooth.
7. Either return to the pan to warm it up before serving.
8. Or serve immediately with the seasoning of your choice.

Nutrition:

Calories: 717.3
Protein: 10.3 g
Fat: 48.3 g
Carbohydrates: 77.4 g

55. White Bean & Spinach Soup

Preparation Time: 10 minutes
Cooking Time: 25 Minutes
Servings: 4

Ingredients:

- 3 cups homemade vegetable broth
- 3 cups cleaned & trimmed baby spinach
- 1 finely diced shallot
- 14.5 oz. white beans can
- 14.5 ounces diced tomatoes
- 1 minced garlic clove
- ½ cup whole wheat shell pasta
- 1 teaspoon rosemary
- 2 teaspoons extra-virgin olive oil
- Red chili flakes as needed
- Black pepper as needed

Directions:

1. Heat oil in a sauce pan before stirring in garlic and diced shallot.
2. Add tomatoes, beans, broth and rosemary. Sprinkle red chili flakes and black pepper for taste.
3. Add pasta and spinach and cook until tender and well-combined.
4. Serve in a bowl with extra seasoning.

Nutrition:

Calories: 218
Protein: 12 g
Fat: 3.3 g
Carbohydrates: 37.9 g

56. Squash Soup With Shredded Apples

Preparation time: 10 minutes
Cooking time: 20 minutes
Servings: 2

Ingredients:
- 2 medium apples
- 2 12oz. plant-based milk
- ¼ teaspoon sea salt
- ½ teaspoon pumpkin spice
- 1 tablespoon extra-virgin olive oil
- 2 16oz. Frozen pureed butternut squash
- ⅛ teaspoon ground black pepper

Directions:
1. Defrost the frozen squash in the microwave.
2. Peel and use a grater to shred apples into thin strips and keep ¼ cup of apples aside.
3. Heat oil in a saucepan over medium heat.
4. Stir in all the apples except ¼ cup and let it cook for 5 minutes until tender.
5. Mix in thawed squash and pumpkin spice.
6. Add 1/2 plant-based milk gradually and stir.
7. Sprinkle salt and pepper.
8. Bring it to a boil over high heat and keep stirring.
9. Serve in bowls with the set aside apples strips on top.

Nutrition:
Calories: 334
Fat: 4 g
Saturated fat: 1 g
Cholesterol: 7 mg
Sodium: 370 mg
Fiber: 5 g
Protein: 18 g
Carbohydrates: 62 g
Potassium: 1,142 mg

57. Lentil & Sweet Potato Soup

Preparation Time: 10 minutes
Cooking Time: 40 minutes
Servings: 6

Ingredients:
- 5 cups of water
- 11 cup red lentils
- 3 onions
- 750g sweet potatoes
- ½ cup chopped coriander
- 2 teaspoons cumin
- 5 garlic cloves
- Sea salt as needed
- Black pepper as needed
- Directions:
- ¼ teaspoon cayenne

Directions:
1. Remove the skin from your onions and sweet potatoes and chop them.
2. Add garlic, water, lentils, turmeric, cayenne and cumin to a pot.
3. Bring it to a boil on high heat and lower it to simmer for 30 minutes or until lentils are done.
4. Use a hand blender to mash them together.
5. Serve with coriander, sea salt and black pepper as needed.

Nutrition:
Calories: 323
Protein: 16 g
Fat: 3.4 g
Carbohydrates: 58.5 g

58. Soy Noodle Soup

Preparation Time: 5 minutes
Cooking Time: 20 minutes
Servings: 4

Ingredients:
- 2 cups of water
- 2 cups soy curls
- 1 cup frozen white onions
- 4 cups vegetable broth
- 2 cups whole-grain rotini pasta
- ¼ cup nutritional yeast
- 1 cup frozen carrots
- 1 teaspoon dried rosemary
- ½ teaspoon ground black pepper

Directions:

1. Take a large sauce pan and add all the ingredients and bring them to a boil over high heat.
2. Lower the heat to a simmer for 15 minutes or until the pasta is softened.
3. Ladle it into bowls and serve hot!

Nutrition:
Calories: 195
Fat: 4g
Fiber: 6.5g
Protein: 14.6g
Carbohydrates: 26.5g

59. Eggplant Tomato Stew

Preparation Time: 5 minutes
Cooking Time: 10 minutes
Servings: 4

Ingredients:
- 1 cup diced onions
- 3 ½ cups cubed eggplants
- 1 cup tomato sauce
- 2 cups diced tomatoes
- ⅛ teaspoon ground cayenne pepper
- 1 teaspoon ground cumin
- 1 teaspoon sea salt
- ½ cup water

Directions:

1. Turn on the instant pot and add all of the ingredients in.
2. Stir to combine and cover the pot
3. Start the manual button and cook for 5 minutes on high setting until done.
4. Once done, let the steam release, carefully open the pot and mix.
5. Serve the stew hot and season with salt if needed.

Nutrition:
Calories: 88
Fat: 1 g
Carbohydrates: 21 g
Protein: 3 g
Fiber: 6g

60. Fulfilling Irish Stew

Preparation Time: 10 minutes
Cooking Time: 20 minutes
Servings: 4

Ingredients:
- 2 peeled and cubed sweet potatoes
- ½ frozen peas
- 4 small & cubed red potatoes
- 15oz. crushed tomatoes can
- 1 teaspoon extra-virgin olive oil
- 1 thinly sliced celery stalk
- 3 peeled and cut into rounds carrots
- 1 small diced onion
- 2 minced garlic cloves
- 1 teaspoon smoked paprika
- 1 teaspoon sea salt
- 1/2 teaspoon dried thyme
- ½ teaspoon black pepper
- 5 cups water

Directions:

1. Heat oil in a large pan over medium heat.
2. Once hot, stir in onion, garlic and cook for 5 minutes or until you can smell the aroma.
3. Put in celery and carrots, stir and cook for 5 minutes.
4. Next, add all the potatoes, tomatoes and water. Stir to mix!
5. Bring it to a boil on high heat.
6. Add in smoked paprika, peas, salt, thyme and black pepper and let simmer on medium heat for 20 minutes until tender and stew is thick.
7. Serve immediately with whole grains if you like.

Nutrition:
Calories: 272
Fat: 2g
Carbohydrates: 55g
Protein: 7g
Fiber: 10g
Sodium: 828 mg

61. Lemon Edamame Stew

Preparation time: 20 minutes
Cooking time: 20 minutes
Servings: 4

Ingredients:
- 35 oz. unsalted diced Italian tomatoes
- 1 cup diced onion

- 1 cup rinsed, quartered and sliced Zucchini
- 16 oz. frozen shelled edamame
- 1 tablespoon extra-virgin olive oil
- ¼ teaspoon ground cayenne pepper
- 1 tablespoon ground cumin
- ½ teaspoon cinnamon
- 1 cup frozen yellow corn
- 5 minced garlic cloves
- ¼ teaspoon sea salt
- 2 tablespoons lemon juice
- ½ teaspoon dried oregano

Directions:
1. Add frozen edamame and water enough to cover in a large pot.
2. Boil over high heat and turn down heat to medium and cook for 5 minutes.
3. Once done, drain the water and set aside.
4. Sauté the onion in a large pan in hot oil over medium heat.
5. Stir for 5 minutes or until translucent.
6. Sauté in cayenne pepper, cumin, cinnamon and stir for 2 minutes.
7. Add garlic, drained edamame, zucchini, tomatoes, corn and salt and stir.
8. Put the lid on and cook for 15 minutes or until zucchini is tender.
9. Mix in oregano and lemon juice.
10. Serve hot immediately!

Nutrition:
Calories 285
Fat 10 g
Saturated fat 1 g
Cholesterol 0 mg
Sodium 303 mg
Fiber 14 g
Protein 16 g
Carbohydrates 40 g
Potassium 1,227 mg

62. Okra Black Eyed Peas Stew
Preparation Time: 10 minutes
Cooking Time: 30 minutes
Servings: 5

Ingredients:
- 1 diced onion
- 1 minced garlic clove
- 1 can crushed tomatoes
- 2 tablespoons extra-virgin olive oil
- 8 oz. frozen & thawed okra
- ¼ teaspoon cayenne
- 2 cans drained black eyed peas
- Sea salt as needed

Directions:
1. Sauté onions in hot oil over medium heat.
2. Once golden brown, sauté in garlic and cayenne for a minute.
3. Combine all of the rest of the ingredients and cook until the okra becomes tender on simmering heat.
4. Serve immediately!

Nutrition:
Calories: 338
Protein: 21 g
Fat: 4 g
Carbohydrates: 58 g

63. Gluten-Free Quinoa Stew
Preparation Time: 10 minutes
Cooking Time: 20 minutes
Servings: 2

Ingredients:
- 1 cubed avocado
- 1 medium chopped onion
- 5 minced garlic cloves
- 1 cubed red bell pepper
- 2 teaspoons coriander
- 6 cups vegetable broth
- 2 teaspoons paprika
- 2 teaspoons cumin
- 1 lbs. cubed red potatoes
- 1 cup frozen corn
- 1 cup washed white quinoa
- 14 oz. diced tomatoes
- 1 cup frozen peas
- Sea salt as needed
- Black pepper as needed
- A handful of fresh cilantro
- 2 tablespoons extra-virgin olive oil

Directions:

1. Heat oil in a large pot over medium heat.
2. Sauté in your onion and bell pepper for 7 minutes until translucent.
3. Mix in paprika, garlic, coriander and cumin for less than a minute.
4. Next, pour in the broth and potatoes.
5. Bring to a boil on high heat and then lower to a simmer for 8 minutes until everything is tender.
6. Mix in the corn and tomatoes for 5 minutes on simmering heat.
7. Add peas and cook for 3 minutes.
8. Remove from stove and sprinkle salt and pepper to taste.
9. Serve in bowls with cilantro and avocado.

Nutrition:

Calories: 398
Carbohydrates: 52g
Protein: 13g
Fat: 17g
Saturated Fat: 4g
Cholesterol: 14mg
Sodium: 1212 mg
Potassium: 1016mg
Fiber: 9g
Sugar: 10

64. Vegan Eggplant Stew

Preparation Time: 15 minutes
Cooking Time: 6 hours
Servings: 6

Ingredients:

- 2 cups vegetable broth
- ¼ cup extra-virgin olive oil
- 1 lbs. chopped tomatoes
- 5 minced garlic cloves
- 1 large diced onion
- 3 lbs. round ¾'-1'cubed eggplant
- 2 teaspoons smoked paprika
- 2 tablespoons tomato paste
- 1 tablespoon ground cumin
- Sea salt as needed
- Black pepper as needed

Directions:

1. Add everything to the slow cooker and cover.
2. Cook it for 6 hours until the eggplant turns tender and the stew thickens.
3. Ladle it in the bowl with salt & pepper if you like.

Nutrition:

Calories: 178
Carbohydrates: 22g
Protein: 4g
Fat: 10g
Saturated Fat: 1g
Sodium: 368 mg
Potassium: 832mg
Fiber: 9g
Sugar: 12g

65. Peanut Butter Stew

Preparation Time: 10 minutes
Cooking Time: 20 minutes
Servings: 4

Ingredients:

- 5 oz. chopped spinach
- 3 lbs. Peeled and cubed sweet potatoes
- 1 large diced onion
- 15oz. diced tomatoes
- ¾ cup natural peanut butter
- 4 cups low-sodium vegetable stock
- 5 minced garlic cloves
- 1 tablespoon ground coriander
- 1 tablespoon extra-virgin olive oil
- 2 tablespoons grated ginger
- 1 diced jalapenos
- Lemon juice from 2 small lemons
- Sea salt as needed
- Black pepper as needed
- Chopped fresh cilantro

Directions:

1. Heat oil in a large pan over medium heat. Sauté in onion, garlic, ginger and jalapenos for 5 minutes or until fragrant.
2. Add all the liquids, sweet potatoes, tomatoes and spices and bring to a boil. Lower heat to a simmer for 15

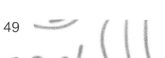

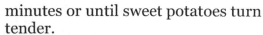

minutes or until sweet potatoes turn tender.

3. Remove from stove and mix in peanut butter, and top with spinach and lemon juice.
4. Allow it to cool, so the soup will thicken.
5. Serve with sea salt and black pepper as needed.

Nutrition:
Calories 276
Fat 17.7g
Saturated Fat 3.5g
Cholesterol 0 mg
Sodium 201.4mg
Carbohydrates 22.3g
Fiber 8.8g
Sugars 7.4g
Protein 15g

66. Cabbage & Beet Stew
Preparation Time: 10 minutes
Cooking Time: 30 minutes
Servings: 4
Ingredients
- 3 cups vegetable stock
- 2 tablespoons fresh lemon juice
- 2 tablespoons extra-virgin olive oil
- ½ cup shredded carrots
- 2 cups shredded cabbage
- ½ teaspoon garlic powder
- 1 cup shredded beets
- ½ teaspoon onion powder
- Sea salt as needed
- Black pepper as needed
- Dill to serve

Directions:
1. Heat up the oil in a pan over medium heat and stir fry all the vegetables.
2. Stir in the stock and add in the seasonings.
3. Reduce to a simmer until everything's cooked.
4. Serve with dill on top and salt & pepper as needed.

Nutrition:
Calories: 95
Protein: 1 g

Fat: 7 g
Carbs: 10 g

67. Delicious Chickpea Sourdough Stew
Preparation Time: 40 minutes
Cooking Time: 30 minutes
Servings: 4
Ingredients:
- 2 tablespoons extra-virgin olive oil
- 1 chopped onion
- 12oz. chickpeas
- 4 chopped garlic cloves
- 2 teaspoons paprika
- 1 tablespoon cumin
- 3 sliced carrots
- 1 lemon juice
- Sourdough round load with top cut out
- 1 teaspoon sea salt

Directions:
1. Place a medium sized saucepan over medium heat and heat the oil.
2. Sauté in garlic, onion and carrots and cover until onions turn translucent.
3. Put in paprika, salt, cumin and stir.
4. In a separate pan, boil chickpeas and leave to simmer for 20 minutes or until soft.
5. Make sure you have added enough water to make stew.
6. Add the garlic, carrots and onion mixture to the pan.
7. Adjust the consistency of the soup with water if you like.
8. Otherwise, serve in a bread bowl with sourdough bread and add lemon juice for extra flavor

Nutrition:
Calories: 149
Carbohydrates: 21g
Protein: 6g
Fat: 6g
Saturated Fat: 1g
Sodium: 855 mg
Potassium: 371mg
Fiber: 6g
Sugar: 4g

68. The Ultimate Vegetable Stew

Preparation Time: 15 minutes
Cooking Time: 30 minutes
Servings: 4

Ingredients:

- 1 medium chopped tomato
- 1 yellow diced onion
- 2 sliced carrots
- 3 chopped garlic cloves
- 1 small potato
- 5 de-stemmed and chopped kale leaves
- 1 cup raw red lentils
- 1 carton vegetable stock
- ½ cup nutritional yeast
- 2 tablespoons balsamic vinegar
- Black pepper as needed
- Sea salt as needed
- 1 tablespoon extra-virgin olive oil

Directions:

1. Heat olive oil in a large pot over medium heat.
2. Sauté in garlic, onion, potato, and carrots for 3 minutes or until tender.
3. Put in red lentils, vegetable stock, kale and tomato. Lentils and vegetables should be submerged in the broth, or use water if needed.
4. Bring to a boil and reduce heat to a simmer and put the lid on.
5. Let it cook for around 40 minutes until all the vegetables are soft and well-combined.
6. Stir in vinegar, nutritional yeast, salt and pepper as needed.
7. Serve hot and enjoy with extra seasoning.

Nutrition:

Calories: 305
Carbohydrates: 56g
Protein: 20g
Fat: 2g
Saturated Fat: 1g
Sodium: 1578 mg
Potassium: 1388mg
Fiber: 19g
Sugar: 7g

Chapter 7: Salads

69. Quick & Easy Potato Salad
Preparation Time: 15 minutes
Cooking Time: 6 minutes
Servings: 6
Ingredients:
- 2 minced garlic cloves
- 2 pounds cleaned, cubed and boiled baby potatoes
- 2 tablespoons finely chopped thyme
- ¼ extra-virgin olive oil
- ½ lemon juice
- Sea salt as needed
- Black pepper as needed
- 2 tablespoons chopped chives
- ¼ cup finely chopped parsley
- 2 teaspoons dijon

Directions:
1. Take a bowl and add olive oil, dijon, garlic, the juice of 1/2 a lemon, and sea salt and pepper as needed.
2. Whisk it together to create a dressing.
3. Add the dressing and the chopped herbs to the boiled potatoes.
4. Give it all a toss to combine the seasoning.
5. Serve immediately!

Nutrition:
Calories: 193
Fat: 9.6g
Saturated Fat 1.4g
Cholesterol: 0 mg
Sodium: 75.3mg
Carbohydrates: 25.2g
Fiber: 3g
Sugars: 2.1g
Protein: 3.2g

70. Quick & Easy Fruit Salad
Preparation Time: 5 minutes
Cooking Time: 15 minutes
Servings: 4
Ingredients:
- 1 tablespoon lemon juice & zest
- 1 tablespoon maple syrup
- 2 cups fresh & cubed pineapple
- ⅛ teaspoon ginger
- 1 cup sliced banana
- 1 cup orange pieces
- ⅛ teaspoon cinnamon
- ⅛ teaspoon cardamom
- 1 cup ripe, diced & juiced mangoes

Directions:
1. Add all the fruits in a large bowl with the spices and lemon juice for extra flavor.
2. Mix to combine and refrigerate for an hour before serving.

Nutrition:
Calories: 276
Protein: 3.1 g
Fat: 12.3 g
Carbs: 39.7 g

71. Crunchy Vegan Broccoli Salad
Preparation Time: 10 minutes
Cooking Time: 15 minutes
Servings: 2
Ingredients:
- 50ml extra-virgin olive oil
- 300g broken into small pieces broccoli florets
- 2 peeled lengthwise carrots
- 50g toasted & chopped cashews
- 50g dried cranberries
- 1 tablespoon caster sugar
- ¼ teaspoon sea salt flakes
- 80ml apple cider vinegar
- 1 red finely sliced onion
- 1 tablespoon maple syrup
- 1 lemon juice & zest

Directions:
1. Heat sugar, vinegar and salt in a small pan and boil until the sugar dissolves.
2. Add the onion and simmer for a minute.
3. Remove from heat, cover and set aside to cool.
4. In a separate bowl, combine carrots, cranberries, broccoli, and cashews.
5. Add the cooled onions and save the liquid.

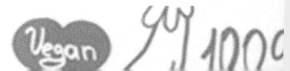

6. Use a whisk to add the liquid in a bowl with lemon juice, maple syrup, and lemon zest.
7. Whisk and pour on the vegetables and combine well.
8. Serve immediately!

Nutrition:
Calories: 617
Fat: 39g
Saturates: 6g
Carbohydrates: 47g
Sugars: 37g
Fiber: 14g
Protein: 13g
Salt: 0.4g

72. Tangy Mango Salad
Preparation Time: 5 minutes
Cooking Time: 5 minutes
Servings: 2
Ingredients:
- ½ peeled small cantaloupe
- 1 cup large peeled, pitted and cut mangos
- 1 Fresh lemon juice
- 1 teaspoon chili powder
- ¼ cup fresh chopped cilantro

Directions:
1. Combine the mango and cantaloupe in a large bowl. Pour the lime juice of one lemon over and top it with the cilantro.
2. Toss gently to combine.
3. Sprinkle chili powder on top before serving.

Nutrition:
Calories: 171
Fat: 1g
Carbohydrates: 42g
Protein: 3g
Fiber: 5g
Sodium: 70mg

73. Smoky Spinach Salad
Preparation Time: 15 minutes
Cooking Time: 5 minutes
Servings: 4

Ingredients:
- 2 tablespoons soy sauce
- 1 ½ tablespoons dijon mustard
- 3 tablespoons pure maple syrup
- ½ teaspoon smoked paprika
- 2 cups sliced strawberries
- 4 cups cut spinach
- ¼ thinly sliced & rinsed onion
- ¼ balsamic vinegar

Directions:
1. Add soy sauce, vinegar, maple syrup, paprika and mustard in a small bowl.
2. Whisk vigorously to combine.
3. Take a large bowl and add in strawberries, spinach and onions.
4. Pour the dressing and toss to combine well.
5. Serve immediately.

Nutrition:
Calories: 84
Fat: 0.7g
Fiber: 2.6g
Protein: 2.2g
Carbohydrates: 18.4g

74. Convenient Edamame Salad
Preparation Time: 15 minutes
Cooking Time: 15 minutes
Servings: 1
Ingredients:
- 1 cup shelled & thawed edamame beans
- ½ cup chopped red onion
- 1 chopped red bell pepper
- 1 cup fresh corn kernels
- 5 fresh & sliced basil leaves
- 5 fresh & sliced mint leaves
- 2 tablespoons fresh lemon juice
- Sea salt as needed
- Black pepper as needed

Directions:
Take a mason jar or any jar with a air-tight seal.
Add all the ingredients and lock the lid.
Shake well to combine and before serving.
Nutrition:
Calories: 299
Protein: 20 g

Fat: 9 g
Carbohydrates: 38 g

75. Radish Lettuce Salad
Preparation Time: 5 minutes
Cooking Time: 10 minutes
Servings: 2
Ingredients:
- 6 sliced radishes
- 1 sliced avocado
- 1 leaves separated lettuce head
- 2 sliced tomatoes
- 3 finely chopped garlic cloves
- ½ peeled & sliced onion
- ½ cup extra-virgin olive oil
- ½ cup apple cider vinegar
- ½ fresh lemon juice
- Sea salt as needed
- Black pepper as needed

Directions:
1. Take a platter and spread your lettuce leaves on it, then put onions, tomatoes, avocado and radishes on it.
2. Make a dressing by combining all the liquid ingredients and garlic. Whisk and adjust the seasoning and drizzle it over your lettuce salad.
3. Serve immediately!

Nutrition:
Calories: 223
Protein: 3g
Fat: 19g
Carbs: 10g

76. Delicious Japanese Style Cucumber Salad
Preparation Time: 5 minutes
Cooking Time: 10 minutes
Servings: 2
Ingredients:
- 3 oz. dried soba noodles
- 1 medium peeled, seeded, halved, and half-mooned sliced cucumber
- 1 tablespoon brown sugar
- 1 teaspoon sea salt
- ⅓ rice vinegar
- ½ hot water
- 1 medium julienned zucchini

- 2 stems thinly sliced scallion
- ½ tablespoon soy sauce
- ¼ cup chopped cilantro

Directions:
1. Take a bowl and add cucumber.
2. In a separate bowl, whisk hot water, sugar, salt, and vinegar,
3. Drizzle it over the cucumber, making sure the cucumber is completely covered.
4. Leave it aside for 15 minutes
5. Take zucchini and add to a large bowl.
6. Boil the soba noodles in a pan of water for 4 minutes until tender.
7. Drain the water when done and add the noodles to the bowl of zucchini and give a mix.
8. Add vinegar, as many cucumber slices as you like, and soy sauce and mix to coat.
9. Throw in the scallions and cilantro and give a good toss.
10. Check the seasonings, adjust the salt and pepper, and serve warm.

Nutrition:
Calories: 112
Carbohydrates: 21g
Protein: 5g
Fat: 1g
Saturated Fat: 1g
Sodium: 1454 mg
Potassium: 438mg
Fiber: 2g
Sugar: 10g
Calcium: 54mg

77. Everyday Bean Salad
Preparation Time: 10 minutes
Cooking Time: 10 minutes
Servings:
Ingredients:
- 1 large diced avocado
- ½ cup diced tomato
- ½ cup diced onion
- 150z. drained & rinsed pinto beans
- 12 oz. drained & rinsed chickpeas
- 150z. drained & rinsed unsalted corn
- 150z. drained & rinsed black beans

- ¼ chopped cilantro
- 3 tablespoons fresh lemon juice
- Sea salt as needed

Directions:
1. Take a large bowl and combine all the ingredients.
2. Serve the salad at room temperature.

Nutrition:
Calories: 474
Carbohydrates: 78g
Protein: 22g
Fat: 12g
Saturated Fat: 2g
Sodium: 996 mg
Potassium: 1340mg
Fiber: 23g
Sugar: 8g
Calcium: 141 mg

78. Citrusy Watercress Salad

Preparation Time: 10 minutes
Cooking Time: 10 minutes
Servings: 4

Ingredients:
- 2 blood oranges
- 1 tablespoon maple syrup
- 2 tablespoons fresh chives
- 3 cups stemless watercress
- 1 tablespoon toasted & chopped hazelnuts
- ⅛ teaspoon sea salt
- 1 tablespoon fresh lemon juice
- 1 tablespoon water
- 1 tablespoon extra-virgin olive oil

Directions:
1. Use a whisk to combine all the liquid ingredients, chives and sea salt.
2. Put in the watercress and toss to coat.
3. Place the salad in bowls and top with orange slices and hazelnuts.
4. Serve immediately!

Nutrition:
Calories: 94
Protein: 2 g
Fat: 5 g
Carbs: 13 g

79. Citrus Kale Salad

Preparation Time: 20 minutes
Cooking Time: 15 minutes
Servings: 4

Ingredients:
- 1 large bundle chopped kale
- 1 tablespoon brown sugar
- 2 tablespoons water
- ¼ thinly sliced red onion
- 1 segmented orange (Reserve any juice)
- 1 cored and chopped apple
- ¼ cup pomegranate arils
- 1 tablespoon dijon mustard
- A pinch of sea salt
- A pinch of black pepper
- ½ tablespoon maple syrup
- 1/3 cup red wine vinegar
- ⅓ cup extra-virgin olive oil
- Hemp seeds for topping

Directions:
1. Take a small bowl and whisk in water, vinegar, water and brown sugar.
2. Add onion to the mix and make sure the onions completely drench in the liquid.
3. Rub the kale with the reserved orange juice and olive oil in a bowl.
4. And put in all the fruits and set aside.
5. In a separate bowl, whisk mustard, maple syrup, vinegar, salt and pepper. Check the taste, whisk in olive oil and adjust the seasoning if needed.
6. Add the onion mix to the kale salad and the dressing. Give a good toss to coat and serve with hemp seeds.

Nutrition:
Calories: 239
Carbohydrates: 21 g
Protein: 2.8 g
Fat: 17 g
Saturated Fat: 2.4 g
Cholesterol: 0 mg
Sodium: 100 mg
Fiber: 3 g
Sugar: 11.7 g

80. Easy Lentil Potato Salad

Preparation Time: 15 minutes
Cooking Time: 10 minutes
Servings: 2

Ingredients:

- 8 cooked & halved potatoes
- ½ cup cooked beluga lentils
- 1 cup thinly sliced scallions
- ¼ cup lemon vinaigrette
- ¼ halved cherry tomatoes
- Sea salt as needed
- Black pepper as needed

Directions:

1. Add lentils to a bowl or serving plate and top with scallions, potatoes, and tomatoes.
2. Drizzle the vinaigrette and sprinkle salt and pepper.
3. Serve immediately!

Nutrition:

Calories: 400
Protein: 7 g
Fat: 26 g
Carbs: 39 g

81. Simple Cucumber Salad

Preparation Time: 5 minutes
Cooking Time: 1 hour 20 minutes
Servings: 4

Ingredients:

- 5 tablespoons apple cider vinegar
- 2 tablespoons white vinegar
- ⅓ cup brown sugar
- ½ cup water
- Sea salt
- 2 medium sliced cucumbers
- Dill as needed
- Black pepper as needed
- Sea salt as needed

Directions:

1. Add sliced cucumbers to a strainer and sprinkle salt over them
2. Let them drain and absorb the salt in the skin.
3. Put water, sugar, and vinegar in a pan over medium heat until sugar dissolves.
4. Remove from the stove and let it cool.
5. Wash the cucumbers to remove the salt.
6. Add to the container and pour the sugar mixture.
7. Give it two hours to set.
8. Serve with dill on top and sprinkle with salt and pepper as needed.

Nutrition:

Calories: 82
Carbohydrates: 19g
Protein: 1g
Fat: 1g
Saturated Fat: 1g
Sodium: 5mg
Potassium: 151mg
Fiber: 1g
Sugar: 18g

82. Red Pepper & Broccoli Salad

Preparation Time: 10 minutes
Cooking Time: 15 minutes
Servings: 2

Ingredients:

- 1 chopped broccoli florets
- 3 tablespoons white wine vinegar
- 1 seeded & chopped red pepper
- 1 Oz. lettuce salad mix
- 1 peeled & finely chopped garlic clove
- 1 teaspoon dijon mustard
- ½ teaspoon black pepper
- 2 tablespoons extra-virgin olive oil
- 1 tablespoon chopped parsley
- Sea salt as needed

Directions:

1. Add your broccoli to boiling water to blanch it and drain.
2. Dry it on a clean kitchen towel.
3. Whisk all the ingredients except broccoli in a bowl.
4. Transfer broccoli to a bowl and drizzle the dressing over it to serve.

Nutrition:

Calories: 185
Protein: 4 g
Fat: 14 g
Carbohydrates: 8 g

83. Easy Cauliflower Salad

Preparation Time: 10 minutes
Cooking Time: 10 minutes
Servings: 4

Ingredients:

- ¼ chopped cilantro
- 1 ½ oz. boiled & drained cauliflower florets
- ¼ cup extra-virgin olive oil
- ¼ teaspoon dried dill
- ½ oregano
- 10 oz. drained canned chickpeas
- 1 teaspoon dried mint
- 1 teaspoon minced garlic
- 2 tablespoons lemon juice
- 1 teaspoon lemon zest
- Sea salt as needed
- Black pepper as needed

Directions:

1. Take a salad and add the ingredients except cilantro.
2. Give a good toss to combine.
3. Top with cilantro and serve chilled.

Nutrition:

Calories: 270
Fat: 16g
Carbohydrates: 26.5g
Protein: 8.7g

84. Vegan Tuna Salad

Preparation Time: 5 minutes
Cooking Time: 10 minutes
Servings: 4

Ingredients:

- ½ cup onion
- 14oz. drained & chopped can hearts of palm
- 15.50z. drained & rinsed chickpeas
- ½ diced celery
- ½ teaspoon sea salt
- ¼ cup vegan mayonnaise
- ¼ teaspoon ground black pepper

Directions:

1. Mash the chickpeas with a masher in a bowl until shredded.
2. Add onion, hearts of palm, celery, mayonnaise, salt and pepper.
3. Toss to combine and coat.

4. Serve in bowls immediately!

Nutrition:

Calories: 214
Fat: 6g
Protein: 9g
Carbohydrates: 35g
Fiber: 8g
Sugar: 1g
Sodium: 765mg

85. Fresh Mint & Watermelon Salad

Preparation Time: 5 minutes
Cooking Time: 5 minutes
Servings: 4

Ingredients:

- 1 tablespoon maple syrup
- 1 lemon juice
- 5 cups cubed watermelon
- ½ ground black pepper
- 1 de-seeded & chopped cucumber
- 1 cup chopped mint
- 2 tablespoons extra-virgin olive oil

Directions:

1. Add cucumber and watermelon to a large bowl.
2. In a separate bowl, using a whisk, add oil, maple syrup, and lemon juice until combined.
3. Drizzle it over salad and mix.
4. Serve with mint on top.

Nutrition:

Calories: 120
Fat: 5 g
Carbohydrates: 18 g
Protein: 2 g
Fiber: 2 g

86. Fresh Zucchini Lemon Salad

Preparation Time: 10 minutes
Cooking Time: 3 hours
Servings: 2

Ingredients:

- 1 sliced into rounds yellow squash
- 1 chopped garlic clove
- 2 tablespoons extra-virgin olive oil
- 1 sliced in rounds zucchini
- 1 lemon juice & zest
- 2 tablespoons fresh basil

- ¼ cup coconut milk
- Sea salt as needed
- Black pepper as needed

Directions:
1. Combine all the ingredients in a bowl and give a good toss.
2. Refrigerate for three hours for it set.
3. Serve cold once done!

Nutrition:
Calories: 159
Protein: 3 g
Fat: 14 g
Carbohydrates: 7 g

87. Vegan Tofu Salad
Preparation Time: 10 minutes
Cooking Time: 10 minutes
Servings: 2

Ingredients:
- 1 teaspoon extra-virgin olive oil
- 1 teaspoon capers
- ¼ vegan mayonnaise
- 2 teaspoons dijon mustard
- 1 small minced garlic clove
- 1 teaspoon fresh lemon juice
- ¼ teaspoon sea salt
- ¼ teaspoon turmeric
- Fresh ground black pepper as needed
- 6 whole-grain bread slices
- 2 tablespoons chopped fresh dill
- 2 tablespoons chopped fresh chives
- Pinches of celery seeds
- 7.5 oz. cut ¼ inch cubes of extra-firm tofu

Directions:
1. Whisk all the ingredients in a small bowl except tofu, dill, chives, bread and celery seeds.
2. Lightly crumble the tofu with your hands and add in the dressing. We need the consistency of an egg salad.
3. Add in dill, celery seed, and chives and mix.
4. Refrigerate before serving.
5. Apply the salad to bread slices, cut in the middle and serve immediately.

Nutrition:
Calories: 175

Fat: 3 g
Cholesterol: 0 mg
Protein: 9.1 g
Carbohydrate: 30.5 g
Sugar: 8.9 g
Fiber: 4.4 g fiber
Sodium: 827 mg
Calcium: 67 mg

88. Tempeh Buffalo Salad
Preparation Time: 10 minutes
Cooking Time: 10 minutes
Servings: 2

Ingredients:
- ¼ cup vegan butter
- 2 tablespoons extra-virgin olive oil
- 8 oz. tempeh
- ¼ cup hot sauce
- 1 chopped bell pepper
- 1 chopped cucumber
- 1 chopped avocado
- 1 chopped tomato
- 1 chopped radish
- 1 chopped purple onion
- A few salad greens
- Buffalo Sauce as needed

Directions:
1. Stir butter and hot sauce in a saucepan over low heat until the butter has melted.
2. Slice the tempeh into 1" squares and into a triangle shape.
3. Sauté tempeh in oil in a skillet until lightly brown.
4. Remove from stove and add in buffalo sauce
5. Toss to combine well.
6. Add the vegetables in the dressing and serve the salad.

Nutrition:
Calories: 423
Sugar: 1 g
Sodium: 422 mg
Fat: 35 g
Saturated Fat: 30 g
Carbohydrates: 12.5 g
Fiber: 8 g
Protein: 22 g

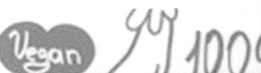

Chapter 8: Rice & Grains

89. Parsley Lemon Pasta

Preparation Time: 5 minutes
Cooking Time: 10 minutes
Servings: 3

Ingredients:

- 3 tablespoons extra-virgin olive oil
- 8.oz long pasta
- ½ cup lemon juice
- 1 teaspoon lemon zest
- 3 minced garlic cloves
- ¼ teaspoon red chili flakes
- Sea salt as needed
- ¼ cup chopped parsley
- Black pepper as needed

Directions:

1. As directed on the package, cook the pasta al dente.
2. Drain the pasta water and save 1/2 cup of pasta water.
3. Run the pasta under cool running water for a moment before setting aside.
4. Heat oil in the pot in which the pasta was cooked.
5. Add the garlic and red pepper flakes, and cook for about a minute.
6. Then, add the pasta and ¼ cup of pasta water, and heat until the pasta is warm.
7. Put the heat on low and add the lemon juice, lemon zest, and parsley.
8. Stir and season with pepper and salt to taste.
9. Serve Immediately!

Nutrition:

Calories: 366
Fat: 9.9g
Saturated Fat: 1.4g
Cholesterol: 0 mg
Sodium: 33.2mg
Carbohydrates: 59.2g
Fiber: 3.4g
Sugars: 0.8g
Protein: 10.1g

90. Fried Pineapple Rice

Preparation Time: 10 minutes
Cooking Time: 30 minutes
Servings: 6

Ingredients:

- 1 tablespoon sesame oil
- 2 tablespoons fresh & chopped cilantro
- ½ cup chopped pineapple
- ½ teaspoon turmeric
- 1 chopped tomato
- 1 teaspoon curry powder
- 1 tablespoon chopped pineapple
- 1 small chopped onion
- 3 cups cooked & cooled brown rice
- 1 tablespoon soy sauce
- Sea salt as needed
- Black pepper as needed

Directions:

1. Add the sesame oil to a saucepan and heat
2. Sauté onions until translucent.
3. Stir in your cooked rice, soy sauce, pineapple, curry powder, and turmeric.
4. Cook for ten minutes while mixing well.
5. Season with salt and pepper and serve with cilantro.

Nutrition

Calories: 179
Protein: 3g
Fat: 4.4g
Carbohydrates: 32.6g

91. Almond Crackers

Preparation Time: 15 minutes
Cooking Time: 15 minutes
Servings: 8

Ingredients:

- 1 tablespoon sesame seeds
- 4 tablespoons water
- 1 cup almond flour
- ½ teaspoon sea salt

- 2 tablespoons flaxseed meal

Directions:
1. Set the oven to 350 degrees Fahrenheit.
2. Prepare a baking sheet with parchment paper.
3. Mix flaxseed meal and water in a small bowl.
4. Leave for 10 minutes, stirring occasionally.
5. After 10 minutes, the mixture should be gooey. It acts as binding agent for the mixture.
6. Combine almond flour, flax mixture, salt, and sesame seeds in a medium bowl.
7. Roll the dough into a ball and place it on a parchment-lined surface.
8. Then, cover again with a piece of parchment paper, press with your hand to flatten.
9. Roll with a pin until it is about 1/8 inch thick.
10. The thinner the crackers, the crispier they will be.
11. Remove cover paper.
12. Using a pizza cutter or knife, cut any shape to your desired size.
13. Poke the center with a toothpick to prevent puffing.
14. Add a little salt if desired.
15. Put the leftover parchment paper on the baking sheet. Put each cracker on the sheet carefully.
16. Bake for 15 minutes or until the edges are slightly golden brown.
17. Allow it to cool and serve.

Nutrition:
Calories: 87
Fat: 2.5g
Saturated Fat: 0g
Cholesterol: 0mg
Sodium: 72.7mg
Carbohydrates: 2.5g
Fiber: 1g
Sugars: 0.5g
Protein: 2.4g

92. Cauliflower Black Bean Rice

Preparation Time: 10 minutes
Cooking Time: 20 minutes
Servings: 4

Ingredients:
- 15.5 oz. cooked black beans
- 3 cups cauliflower rice
- ½ cup chopped onion
- 1 ½ teaspoon minced garlic
- ¼ teaspoon ground cayenne pepper
- ½ cup diced red bell pepper
- 3 tablespoons chopped pickled jalapeno
- ¼ teaspoon ground black pepper
- ⅓ teaspoon sea salt
- 2 tablespoons extra-virgin olive oil
- ½ cup diced parsley

Directions:
1. Add oil and garlic in a large skillet over medium heat and cook for 2 minutes.
2. Sauté onion and red bell pepper, seasoning with all spices.
3. Cook it for 5 minutes, and sauté in cauliflower rice and jalapeno.
4. Add salt and black pepper, cook for 7 minutes while stirring.
5. Add beans and cook them for 2 minutes until hot.
6. Serve topped with parsley

Nutrition:
Calories: 270.3
Fat: 1.6 g
Carbohydrates: 52.7 g
Protein: 13.5
Fiber: 13.1 g

93. Chard Wraps With Millet

Preparation Time: 5 minutes
Cooking Time: 10 minutes
Servings: 4

Ingredients:
- 1 cut into thin strips carrot
- ½ cut into thin strips cucumber
- ½ cup cooked chickpeas
- ½ cooked millet
- 1 cup sliced cabbage
- Hemp seeds as needed

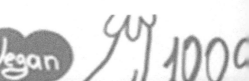

- 1 bunch swiss rainbow chard
- Mint leaves as needed
- ⅓ cup hummus

Directions:
1. Apply hummus on one side of chard, put some millet, veggies, and chickpeas.
2. Add mint leaves and hemp seeds as a topping and turn it into a burrito.
3. Serve immediately!

Nutrition:
Calories: 152
Fat: 4.5 g
Carbohydrates: 25 g
Protein: 3.5 g
Fiber: 2.4 g

94.Corn Kernel Black Bean Rice
Preparation Time: 10 minutes
Cooking Time: 25 minutes
Servings: 8
Ingredients:
- 15.25 oz. cooked kernel corn
- 8 oz. yellow rice mix
- 2 tablespoons extra-virgin olive oil
- 1 teaspoon ground cumin
- 1 1/4 cups water
- 15 oz. cooked black beans
- 2 teaspoons lemon juice

Directions:
1. Heat a saucepan over high heat by adding oil, water and rice.
2. Bring it to a boil and reduce heat to medium.
3. Let it simmer until rice is tender and the liquid has vanished.
4. Place the rice in a large bowl.
5. Add the rest of the ingredients to the rice.
6. Mix to combine and serve immediately!

Nutrition:
Calories: 100
Fat: 4.4 g
Carbohydrates: 15.1 g
Protein: 2 g
Fiber: 1.4 g

95.Rice & Cuban Beans
Preparation Time: 20 minutes
Cooking Time: 55 Minutes
Servings: 6
Ingredients:
- 2 ½ cups vegetable broth
- 1 cup uncooked rice
- 1 cup chopped onion
- 1 teaspoon sea salt
- 1 teaspoon minced garlic
- 4 tablespoons tomato paste
- 1 cored & chopped green bell pepper
- 15.25 oz. cooked kidney beans
- 1 tablespoon extra-virgin olive oil

Directions:
1. Heat oil in a saucepan over medium heat.
2. Add onion, garlic, bell pepper and sauté for 5 minutes until tender.
3. Sauté in tomato and salt and cook for a minute.
4. Mix in the rice and beans, pour in the stock and stir.
5. Cook for 45 minutes or until the liquid has absorbed.
6. Serve hot!

Nutrition:
Calories: 258
Fat: 3.2g
Carbohydrates: 49.3g
Protein: 7.3g
Fiber: 5g

96. Potato & Corn Chowder
Preparation Time: 10 minutes
Cooking Time: 16 minutes
Servings: 6
Ingredients:
- 2 medium peeled & chopped carrots
- 1 ribs chopped celery
- 1 medium peeled onion
- 1 tablespoon extra-virgin olive oil
- ¼ cup all-purpose flour
- 1 teaspoon dried thyme
- 1 ½ teaspoon minced garlic
- 2 cups vegetable broth
- 4 cups chopped white potatoes
- 2 cups vegetable broth

- 3 tablespoons nutritional yeast
- 1 cup frozen corn kernels
- 2 cups unsweetened almond milk
- 1 teaspoon sea salt
- ¼ teaspoon ground black pepper

Directions:
1. Heat oil in a large pot over medium heat.
2. Add onion, garlic, carrots, celery and cook for 5 minutes until golden-brown.
3. Sprinkle thyme and flour and stir to coat for a minute or until the flour turns brown.
4. Next, add yeast, milk, potatoes, vegetable stock and stir until combined.
5. Cook for 8 minutes or until tender.
6. Lastly, add corn and sprinkle sea salt and black pepper.
7. Serve hot!

Nutrition:
Calories: 126
Fat: 3 g
Carbohydrates: 18 g
Protein: 6 g
Fiber: 3 g

97. Tomato Pesto Quinoa
Preparation Time: 10 minutes
Cooking Time: 25 minutes
Servings: 1
Ingredients:
- 2 tablespoons sun dried chopped tomatoes
- 1 cup chopped onion
- 1 minced garlic clove
- A pinch of sea salt
- 1 cup chopped zucchini
- 1 chopped tomato
- 3 tablespoons Basil Pesto
- 2 cups cooked Quinoa
- 1 cup chopped spinach
- 1 tablespoon nutritional yeast

Directions:
1. Heat oil in a skillet over medium heat.
2. Add onion and garlic and cook for 5 minutes until translucent.

3. Add in zucchini and sea salt, and cook for 5 minutes.
4. Next, put in sun dried tomatoes and combine well.
5. Stir in the pesto and combine well.
6. Put spinach, quinoa and zucchini mixture in a bowl or plate, and serve with nutritional yeast.

Nutrition:
Calories: 535
Protein: 20g
Fat: 23g
Carbohydrates: 69g

98. Oatmeal Cookies
Preparation Time: 10 minutes
Cooking Time: 25 minutes
Servings: 12
Ingredients:
- 2 cups oatmeal
- ½ teaspoon cinnamon
- ⅓ cup raisins
- ¼ cup applesauce
- ⅓ teaspoon pure vanilla extract
- 1 cup mashed ripe banana

Directions:
1. Preheat oven to 350 degrees Fahrenheit.
2. Combine everything to a gooey consistency.
3. Spoon it on an ungreased baking sheet and then apply pressure to flatten.
4. Bake for fifteen minutes or until done.
5. Allow it to cool on a baking wire and serve!

Nutrition:
Calories: 79.1
Protein: 2g
Fat: 1g
Carbohydrates: 16.4g

99. No-Bake Peanut Butter Oat Bars
Preparation Time: 10 minutes
Cooking Time: 10 minutes
Servings: 20
Ingredients:
- ½ cup maple syrup

- 2 cups gluten free oats
- ¾ cup creamy peanut butter
- ¼ cup pepitas
- 2 tablespoons cacao nibs
- 4oz. vegan chopped dark chocolate bar
- 1 tablespoon coconut oil
- 3 tablespoons hemp hearts
- ¼ cup shredded & unsweetened coconut flakes
- A pinch of sea salt

Directions:
1. Use parchment paper to line an 8inchx8inch baking sheet.
2. Place a saucepan on low heat with peanut butter and maple syrup
3. Cook and stir until well combined.
4. Remove from stove when done.
5. In a skillet, add oats and pepitas and toast on low heat for 5 minutes
6. Put the oats and peanut butter mixture in a mixing bowl with hemp hearts and cacao nibs stirred well.
7. Pour the mixture onto the lined baking sheet and use a glass to press down the mixture firmly into the dish until no cracks.
8. Let chill in the fridge.
9. Melt chocolate and coconut oil in a double boiler, or use the microwave.
10. Toast coconut flakes in the pan in which the oats were toasted.
11. Take out the peanut butter mixture from the fridge and pour chocolate over it.
12. Refrigerate for half an hour or until firm.
13. Season with salt before cutting the bars.
14. Store them in the fridge and serve however you like.

Nutrition:
Calories: 170
Sugar: 8 g
Sodium: 158 mg
Fat: 7.5 g
Saturated Fat: 3 g
Carbohydrates: 21 g

Fiber: 3 g
Protein: 4.5 g
Cholesterol: 0 mg

100. Peanut Butter Rice Crispy Treats
Preparation Time: 5 minutes
Cooking Time: 35 minutes
Servings: 6
Ingredients:
- 1 cup brown rice syrup
- ⅓ cup cacao nibs
- 5 cups rice crispy cereal
- 1 cup natural peanut butter
- 1 teaspoon coconut oil

Directions:
1. Prepare a 9 x 9 square pan with parchment paper.
2. You may also grease with coconut oil
3. Place a large pan on low heat and carefully heat up brown rice syrup and peanut butter while stirring.
4. Take off from stove and mix in the rice crispy cereal until combined. Stir in the cacao nibs well.
5. Put the mixture in the lined square pan and carefully put pressure until evenly distributed.
6. Cut into squares and serve. Or chill for 30 minutes in the fridge before serving.

Nutrition:
Calories: 359
Fat: 17.6g
Saturated Fat: 4.6g
Cholesterol: 0.2mg
Sodium: 259.8mg
Carbohydrates: 46.1g
Fiber: 2.2g
Sugars: 27g
Protein: 7.9g

101. Creamy Mushroom Stroganoff
Preparation time: 10 minutes
Cooking Time: 20 minutes
Servings: 4
Ingredients:
- 1 small finely diced yellow onion
- 3 minced garlic cloves

- 4 tablespoons extra-virgin olive oil
- 2 tablespoons whole-wheat flour
- 2 lbs. trimmed & sliced cremini mushrooms
- ¾ cup dry white wine
- ¾ vegan sour cream
- 1 ¼ cup low-sodium vegetable stock
- 2 tablespoons chopped parsley
- Sea salt as needed
- Black pepper as needed
- 16 oz. whole-wheat pasta

Directions:
1. As directed on the package, cook the noodles until they are al dente. Drain and reserve ½ cup of pasta water
2. Over medium-high heat, melt butter in a medium pot. Add onion and sauté for 5 minutes until golden.
3. Add garlic and mushrooms, and cook for an additional five minutes until the mushrooms become tender.
4. Stir in the flour, ensuring there are no white streaks, for a minute.
5. Add in the wine and vegetable stock on a medium flame and cook for 5 minutes or until the sauce has thickened.
6. Mix in the sour cream and sprinkle salt and pepper as needed
7. Put pasta in the mushroom sauce and give a toss to combine. Use the pasta water if needed to make the sauce more liquid.
8. Serve in bowls with creamy sauce on top

Nutrition:
Calories: 447
Fat: 14g
Saturated Fat: 2.2g
Cholesterol: 0mg
Sodium: 127.8mg
Carbohydrates: 66.7g
Fiber: 4.2g
Sugars: 5.6g
Protein: 15.2g

102. Easy Chickpea Tacos
Preparation Time: 20 minutes
Cooking Time: 20 minutes
Servings: 2
Ingredients:
- 1 tablespoon tamari
- 2 teaspoons garlic powder
- 1 ½ cups drained & rinsed cooked chickpeas
- ½ teaspoon cumin
- ½ teaspoon onion powder
- ½ teaspoon paprika
- 1/1 cup cilantro
- 2 thinly sliced green onions
- ½ sliced avocado
- 1 tablespoon Sriracha hot sauce
- ¼ shredded head cabbage
- 2 thinly sliced green onions
- Vegan sour cream
- Lime wedges

Directions:
1. Add chickpeas, garlic, onion powder, cumin, paprika, tamari, and hot sauce in a small pan.
2. Heat the mixture over medium heat and remove once done.
3. Warm the tortillas on the stove until slightly charring on the edges. Keep warm in the pot!
4. Top each tortilla with the chickpea mixture, cabbage, green onions, avocado, cilantro and some vegan cream
5. Serve warm with lime wedges!

Nutrition:
Calories: 362
Total Fat: 14.1g
Saturated Fat: 1.9g
Cholesterol: 0 mg
Sodium: 1207.1mg
Carbohydrates: 52.6g
Fiber: 14.5g
Sugars 0.8g
Protein 12g

103. Instant & Yummy Steel Cut Oats

Preparation Time: 1 minute
Cooking Time: 20 minutes

Ingredients:

- 2 ½ cups water
- A pinch of salt
- 1 cup steel cut oats
- 1 teaspoon vanilla
- 2 tablespoons maple syrup
- A handful of berries
- 2 tablespoons of any favorite nuts
- ¼ unsweetened almond milk

Directions:

1. In the Instant Pot insert, combine the steel cut oats, spices, vanilla, and water.
2. Lock the lid by twisting it. Put the valve in the sealed position. Adjust the pressure manually to high for 4 minutes. Then let natural release for 15 minutes.
3. Serve this with nuts and berries, pure maple syrup and almond milk in individual bowls.

Nutrition:

Calories: 150
Protein 5g
Carbohydrates 27g
Fiber: 4g
Sugars: 2g
Fat: 2.5g
Saturated fat: 5g

104. Simple Gluten-Free Bread

Preparation Time: 1 hour 30 minutes
Cooking Time: 1 hour 15 minutes
Servings: 12

Ingredients:

- 2 cups warm water
- 1 packet active dry yeast
- 2 tablespoons organic cane sugar
- Avocado oil
- ¼ ground chia seeds
- ¾ cup gluten-free oat flour
- 1 cup brown rice flour
- ¾ cup sorghum flour
- 1 cup potato starch
- 2 teaspoons sea salt

Directions:

1. Grease and flour an 8 x 4-inch loaf pan with oil and brown rice flour.
2. Whisk the sugar and warm water together in a medium mixing bowl until the sugar dissolves.
3. Stir in the yeast and let it rise on the counter for 10 minutes. In case it doesn't, try again - it could be too hot water or an expired yeast packet.
4. Whisk in the ground chia seeds once the yeast has risen and set it aside for 10 minutes.
5. Take a large bowl and whisk all the flours, potato starch and sea salt.
6. Add the wet ingredients in the middle and mix together with a wooden spatula.
7. The batter should be thick and sticky.
8. Transfer the batter to your greased pan and cover with a kitchen towel.
9. Put it in a warm and enclosed space for an hour to rise even more.
10. Pre-heat the oven to 425 F once the batter has doubled in size.
11. Bake for 45 minutes, then switch the temperature 375 F for 30 minutes.
12. Take the bread out of the oven and let it cool for 10 minutes in the pan.
13. Let cool completely before slicing and serving.

Nutrition:

Calories: 167
Carbohydrates: 35.6 g
Protein: 2.8 g
Fat: 1.7 g
Saturated Fat: 0.3 g
Cholesterol: 0 mg
Sodium: 392 mg
Potassium: 102 mg
Fiber: 2.4 g
Sugar: 2.3 g

105. Vegan Bean Quesadilla

Preparation Time: 10 minutes
Cooking Time: 15 minutes
Servings: 4

Ingredients:
- 1 avocado
- 4 tortillas
- ¼ cup vegetable broth
- ¼ teaspoon cumin
- ¼ teaspoon chili powder
- ¼ teaspoon garlic powder
- ¼ teaspoon onion powder
- 1 adobo chipotle pepper
- 15oz. rinsed & drained pinto beans

Directions
1. Add all the ingredients in a food processor or blender.
2. Process until creamy and use more broth if needed for desired consistency.
3. Layer the mixture on the side of the tortilla, fold it, and put it on a non-stick pan.
4. Cook both sides until brown.
5. Take off from heat, cut and serve!

Nutrition:
Calories: 179
Carbohydrates: 21g
Protein: 4g
Fat: 10g
Saturated Fat: 2g
Sodium: 272 mg
Potassium: 299mg
Fiber: 5g
Sugar: 3g

106. Easy Quinoa Sweet Potato Chili
Preparation Time: 10 minutes
Cooking Time: 35 minutes
Servings: 4
Ingredients:
- 3 medium cubed sweet potatoes
- 2 teaspoons ground cumin
- 1 tablespoon extra-virgin olive oil
- 1 diced yellow or white onion
- ½ teaspoon chipotle powder
- 3 teaspoons hot sauce
- ½ teaspoon ground cinnamon
- 1 tablespoon chili powder
- 16 ounces salsa
- 15 ounces black beans
- 2 cups cooked quinoa

- 2 cups vegetable broth
- 2 cups water
- 1 avocado
- Sea salt as needed
- Black pepper as needed

Directions:
1. Heat the oil in a large pot over medium heat. Combine the onions and a pinch of salt and pepper.
2. Then stir in the cumin, cinnamon, sweet potatoes, chipotle powder, hot sauce, chili powder.
3. After 3 to 4 minutes, add the salsa, vegetable stock, and water.
4. On medium heat, bring the pot to a low boil and then let it simmer.
5. Add black beans let it cook with a lid on for 20 minutes or until the sweet potatoes are fork-tender and the liquid has thickened.
6. Stir in the quinoa at the end.
7. Serve with avocado and enjoy!

Nutrition:
Calories: 525
Carbohydrates: 89g
Protein: 17g
Fat: 14g
Saturated Fat: 2g
Sodium: 1853 mg
Potassium: 1729 mg
Fiber: 22g
Sugar: 15g

107. Easy Tomato Basil Pasta
Preparation Time: 10 minutes
Cooking Time: 45 minutes
Servings: 6
Ingredients:
- ¾ teaspoon sea salt
- ½ cup extra-virgin olive oil
- 1 small chopped cherry tomato basket
- 2 finely chopped garlic cloves
- 1 oz. vegan pasta
- ½ cup chopped fresh basil
- Salt & pepper as needed

Directions:
1. Mix garlic, olive oil and salt in a bowl.

2. Add 1 cup of chopped cherry tomatoes to the olive oil bowl.
3. Allow it to rest for half an hour while stirring often.
4. Cook the pasta according to the guidelines.
5. Drain and reserve ½ pasta water.
6. Mix pasta and tomato mixture. Serve with basil, a little pasta water for consistency, and salt & pepper.

Nutrition:
Calories: 448
Carbohydrates: 58g
Protein: 10g
Fat: 19g
Saturated Fat: 3g
Sodium: 300mg
Potassium: 261mg
Fiber: 3g
Sugar: 3g

108. Simple & Vegan Mexican Style Rice

Preparation Time: 10 minutes
Cooking Time: 20 minutes
Servings: 4

Ingredients:
- 1 teaspoon sea salt
- ½ teaspoon black pepper
- 8oz.can tomato sauce
- 1 ½ cups water
- ¼ of a diced yellow onion
- 2 minced garlic cloves
- ½ tablespoon extra-virgin olive oil
- 1 cup brown rice

Directions:
1. Warm the vegetable oil in a medium saucepan.
2. Add the uncooked rice and sauté until golden.
3. Add the onion and garlic and cook until translucent.
4. Add the tomato sauce and water, as well as salt and pepper.
5. Bring water to a boil, cover the pan, and lower the heat.
6. Cook for 20 minutes.
7. Serve when done with extra seasoning.

Nutrition:
Calories: 203
Carbohydrates: 41g
Protein: 4g
Fat: 2g
Saturated Fat: 2g
Sodium: 886 mg
Potassium: 260mg
Fiber: 2g
Sugar:3g

Chapter 9: Legumes

109. Vegan Adzuki Beans With Rice
Preparation Time: 10 minutes
Cooking Time: 25 minutes
Servings: 6
Ingredients:
- 3 tablespoons tamari
- 1 tablespoon toasted sesame oil
- ¼ cup white miso
- ⅓ cup rice vinegar
- ¼ cup extra-virgin olive oil
- 1 cup sliced sugar snap peas
- 2 tablespoons sesame seeds
- 1 cup cooked brown rice
- 2 tablespoons chopped fresh cilantro
- 3 peeled small carrots
- 1 1/2 cups drained, rinsed & cooked adzuki beans
- 2 sliced avocados
- 1 small sliced fresh red chili
- 1/2 large sliced Napa cabbage head

Directions:
1. Take a bowl and whisk rice vinegar, miso, olive oil, sesame oil and tamari.
2. In a separate bowl, mix carrots, peas, sesame seeds, cabbage and ¼ cup dressing.
3. Before serving, add cilantro to the salad. Separate rice, salad, beans and avocados into four bowls and use more dressing to your liking.
4. Save for later as well.

Nutrition:
Calories: 329
Fat: 1.6g
Saturated fat: 0.3g
Carbohydrates: 67.9g
Sugar: 7.1g
Fiber: 13.7g
Protein: 14.4g
Cholesterol: 0.0g

110. Berbere-Spiced Red Lentils
Preparation Time: 5 minutes
Cooking Time: 25 minutes

Servings: 4
Ingredients:
- 1 teaspoon sea salt
- 2 teaspoons tomato paste
- 1 teaspoon extra-virgin olive oil
- 2 minced garlic cloves
- 1 cup rinsed dried red lentils
- 3 cups water
- 3 chopped tomatoes
- 2 tablespoons berbere spice
- ½ medium finely chopped yellow onion

Directions:
1. Add lentils and water to a saucepan and bring to a boil over high heat.
2. Reduce to medium heat and cook for 20 minutes.
3. In a skillet placed over medium heat, add olive oil, garlic and onion. Stir until fragrant!
4. Add tomatoes, sea salt, tomato paste and berbere spice to it.
5. Cook for 5 minutes or until the mixture becomes deep-red and thick. Leave it aside.
6. Add the tomato mixture to the lentils and let simmer until everything's well-combined, for about 5 minutes.
7. Serve hot immediately!

Nutrition:
Calories: 216
Fat: 3g
Carbohydrates: 38g
Protein: 13g
Fiber: 8g
Sodium: 594mg

111. Creamy Curried Potatoes & Peas
Preparation Time: 15 minutes
Cooking Time: 30 minutes
Servings: 4
Ingredients:
- 1 small cut into ¼-inch pieces yellow onion
- 3 teaspoons curry powder

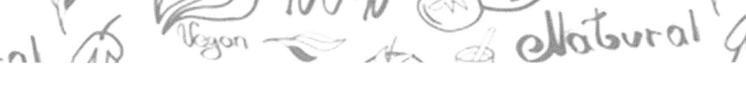

- 3 tablespoons tomato paste
- 1 teaspoon sea salt
- 1 cup frozen peas
- Black pepper as needed
- ¼ cup chopped fresh cilantro
- 2 cups water
- 1 tablespoon extra-virgin olive oil
- 1 lbs. Small diced red potatoes
- 3 minced garlic cloves
- 1 peeled & minced fresh ginger piece

Directions:
1. Heat oil in a wok over medium heat.
2. Stir in potatoes until they start changing their color to brown for 10 minutes.
3. Use the spoon to push the potatoes to one side of the wok, while you throw in ginger, garlic, onion.
4. Cook for 5 minutes or until fragrant.
5. Then combine the potatoes with the rest.
6. Mix water and curry powder in the wok and bring to a boil over high heat.
7. Lower the heat to a simmer and cook until the potatoes turn tender.
8. Add in tomato paste, peas, sea salt and cook while stirring occasionally until the liquid thickens and feels creamy.
9. Check the taste to adjust the seasoning
10. Serve with fresh cilantro on top.

Nutrition:
Calories: 323
Fat: 4g
Carbohydrates: 65g
Protein: 9g
Fiber: 9g
Sodium: 654 mg

112. Chickpea & Cauliflower Fajitas
Preparation Time: 10 minutes
Cooking Time: 30 minutes
Servings: 4
Ingredients:
- 1 teaspoon chili powder
- ½ teaspoon smoked paprika

- 1 seeded & thinly sliced red bell pepper
- 15oz. drained & rinsed chickpeas
- ½ large head cauliflower florets
- 1 small thinly sliced yellow onion
- 1 tablespoon extra-virgin olive oil
- ½ teaspoon garlic powder
- 1 pitted, peeled, quartered, & thinly sliced avocado
- ½ bunch chopped cilantro
- 1 teaspoon sea salt
- 12 (6-inch) soft corn tortillas

Directions:
1. Heat the oil in a large sauté pan over medium heat.
2. Cook the cauliflower for about 5 minutes, or until it starts to brown.
3. Stirring occasionally, cook the onion for 5 minutes.
4. Stir in the bell pepper and cook until the cauliflower is tender
5. Stir in the chickpeas, chili powder, smoked paprika, garlic powder, and salt.
6. Cook and stir for 5 minutes or until you can smell the aroma.
7. Put the mixture in a bowl.
8. Clean the pan you used for the fajita mixture with a kitchen towel and warm it for tortillas.
9. Cook tortillas over medium heat until each side is slightly golden-born.
10. Divide the mixture among tortillas and serve with avocados and cilantro on top.

Nutrition:
Calories: 500
Fat: 18g
Carbohydrates: 73g
Protein: 15g
Fiber: 13g
Sodium: 1,023 mg

113. Chipotle Whole-Wheat Toast
Preparation Time: 10 minutes
Cooking Time: 15 minutes
Servings: 4

Ingredients:
- 2 slices whole-wheat toast
- ¼ teaspoon chipotle spice
- 1 can black beans
- A pinch of sea salt
- 1 freshly juiced lemon
- 1 freshly diced avocado
- ½ freshly diced tomato
- Fresh cilantro
- ¼ cup corn
- 3 tablespoons finely diced onion
- A pinch of black pepper
- 1 teaspoon garlic powder

Directions:
1. Combine chipotle spice with garlic powder, sea salt, beans, and pepper with lemon juice stirred in.
2. Boil this mixture until you have a thick consistency.
3. In a separate bowl, combine tomato, avocado, onion, leftover lemon juice, and corn. Season with salt and pepper.
4. Toast the bread and apply the beans mixture.
5. Serve with a corn salad with cilantro and avocado on top.

Nutrition:
Calories: 290
Fats 9 g
Carbohydrates 44 g
Proteins 12 g

114. Instant Pot Pinto Beans
Preparation Time: 5 minutes
Cooking Time: 1 hour
Servings: 6
Ingredients:
- 4 minced garlic cloves
- ½ diced yellow onion
- 8 cups water
- ½ teaspoon sea salt
- 3 cups of dry pinto beans

Direction:
1. Add beans, water, salt, onion and garlic to a 6-quart pressure cooker.
2. Cook on high pressure for 25 minutes.
3. Release the pressure after 25 minutes and take off the lid.
4. Press the sauté function to cook them another half an hour or until they become soft.
5. Stir in between and serve hot.

Nutrition:
Calories: 342
Carbohydrates: 62g
Protein: 21g
Fat: 1g
Saturated Fat: 1g
Sodium: 222 mg
Potassium: 1373 mg
Fiber: 15g
Sugar: 3g

115. Black Bean and Onion Pilaf
Preparation Time: 15 minutes
Cooking Time: 25 minutes
Servings: 4
Ingredients:
- 1 tablespoon extra-virgin olive oil
- 2 garlic cloves minced
- 5 sliced cremini mushrooms
- 1 thinly sliced carrot
- ½ teaspoon sea salt
- ½ teaspoon chili powder
- 1 medium chopped red onion
- 1 cup of brown rice
- ½ cup chopped green onions
- 1 cup chopped kale
- 2 cups of vegetable broth
- 15oz. Drained & rinsed black beans
- 1 teaspoon fresh lemon juice

Directions:
1. Add oil and sauté onion, mushrooms, carrot, pepper and garlic in a skillet for 3 minutes.
2. Put rice and mix for 30 seconds until shiny.
3. Bring it to a boil by adding vegetable stock and reducing the heat to a simmer.
4. Let the rice cook for 30 minutes until the liquid has vanished.

5. Throw in kale along with cooked black beans, chili powder, sea salt and lemon juice.
6. Give a stir and let it all get a steam for three minutes.
7. Serve with chopped red onion on top.

Nutrition:
Calories: 348
Carbohydrates: 63g
Protein: 13g
Fat: 5g
Saturated Fat: 1g
Sodium: 1190mg
Potassium: 754mg
Fiber: 11g
Sugar: 4g

116. Vegan Yellow Split Peas
Preparation Time: 15 minutes
Cooking Time: 25 minutes
Servings: 4
Ingredients:
- 1 ½ cups chopped broccoli
- 1 cup diced zucchini
- 1 inch minced ginger piece
- 1 minced jalapeno
- 1 cup yellow split peas
- 3 ½ cups vegetable broth
- ½ tablespoons extra-virgin olive oil
- 1 small diced yellow onion
- 5 minced garlic cloves
- 1 tablespoon turmeric paste
- 1/2 Tablespoons of cooking oil

Directions:
1. Heat the oil and turmeric paste over medium heat in a large pan with a lid.
2. Sauté the onion for 5 minutes or until it becomes soft and translucent.
3. Put in the garlic, ginger, and jalapeno, and cook for another minute or two.
4. Combine the broccoli, zucchini, split peas and vegetable broth
5. After bringing the broth to a boil, cover it with a lid, and cook for 30 minutes.
6. Turn up the heat if there is still broth in the pan when you remove the lid

and stir continuously until the broth evaporates and it thickens.
7. You can serve this with rice if you like.

Nutrition:
Calories: 306k
Carbohydrates: 44g
Protein: 16g
Fat: 9g
Saturated Fat: 1g
Trans Fat: 1g
Sodium: 1157mg
Potassium: 427mg
Fiber: 12g

117. Cashew Cheese Mushroom Pea Farro
Preparation Time: 10 minutes
Cooking Time: 20 minutes
Servings: 2
Ingredients:
- 1 large thinly sliced leek
- 5oz. sliced baby portabella mushrooms
- 1 ¼ cups vegetable stock
- ¾ cup quick cooking farro
- ½ cup cashew cheese
- ½ cup thawed frozen peas
- 1 teaspoon extra-virgin olive oil

Directions:
1. Bring vegetable stock to a boil in a medium pot, then add quick cooking farro.
2. Follow the instructions on the package.
3. Heat olive oil in a skillet over medium-high heat.
4. Sauté leeks and mushrooms for 5-7 minutes until soft and fragrant.
5. Add the thawed frozen peas and the farro
6. Mix then add the cashew cheese and give a toss to combine.
7. Top with additional cashew cheese if you like before serving.

Nutrition:
Calories: 275
Carbohydrates: 28g
Protein: 17g

Fat: 13g
Fiber: 5g
Sugar: 7g

118. **Easy Black Beans Rice**
Preparation Time: 10 minutes
Cooking Time: 40 minutes
Servings: 2
Ingredients:
- 1 diced large onion
- 1 diced red pepper
- 1 diced green pepper
- 2 15oz. can drained & rinsed black beans,
- 1 14oz. can drained & rinsed diced tomatoes
- 2 garlic cloves
- 1 bay leaf
- Brown rice
- 1 tablespoon ground cumin
- 1 seeded & diced jalapeno
- ¼ cup apple cider vinegar
- Sea salt as needed
- Black pepper as needed
- Water as needed

Directions:
1. Sauté onions, peppers, and garlic until the onions and peppers are soft.
2. Add the bay leaf and cumin next.
3. Stir in tomatoes, jalapenos, vinegar and beans
4. Allow it to simmer for 5 minutes.
5. Put water that sits above the ingredients.
6. Bring to a boil
7. Reduce heat to a simmer and cook for 30 minutes or until the bean mixture thickens.
8. Remove the bay leaf before serving
9. Add salt & pepper to season and serve immediately with brown rice.

Nutrition:
Calories: 216
Carbohydrates: 40g
Protein: 4g
Fat: 4g
Sodium: 434mg

119. **Quick Sauteed Snap Peas**
Preparation Time: 5 minutes
Cooking Time: 5 minutes
Servings: 4
Ingredients:
- 2 teaspoons olive oil
- 2 teaspoons nutritional yeast
- ½ teaspoon black cracked pepper
- ⅛ teaspoon cayenne pepper
- 500g destemmed & string removed fresh sugar snap peas
- 1 teaspoon sea salt

Directions:
1. Heat oil in a large pan over medium-high heat.
2. Put snap peas and nutritional yeast.
3. Toss in the pan to coat in the oil/yeast mixture.
4. Add salt, pepper, and cayenne as needed.
5. Sauté for about 4-5 minutes or until crisp-tender
6. Put in a serving bowl
7. Season with sea salt and pepper to serve.

Nutrition:
Calories: 84
Carbohydrates: 9g
Protein: 3g
Fat: 4g
Saturated Fat: 2g
Fiber: 3g
Sugar: 4g

120. **Quick Instant Pot Chickpeas**
Preparation Time: 5 minutes
Cooking Time: 40 minutes
Servings: 4
Ingredients:
- 4 cups water
- 1 teaspoon sea salt
- 2 cups chickpeas
- 1 4-inch kombu piece
- 1 garlic clove
- 2 bay leaves
- ½ chunk onion

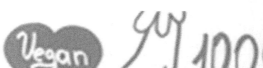

Directions

1. Put chickpeas, onion, bay leaves and garlic clove in the bottom of the insert of a pressure cooker.
2. Add water overtop.
3. Put the lid on, set to lock, and turn the valve to sealing.
4. Manually set the pot to high pressure and let cook for 45 minutes.
5. Once cooked, let the steam release itself, it will take 15 minutes.
6. Turn the valve to the venting option to complete the process.
7. Remove the onion, bay leaf, and garlic.
8. Serve with brown rice and kombu, or enjoy as a side dish.

Nutrition:

Calories: 67
Fat 1.5g
Saturated Fat 0.2g
Cholesterol 0mg
Sodium 338.1mg
Total Carbohydrate 10.2g
Fiber 3.3g
Sugars 0g
Protein 3.7g

121. **Quick Instant Pot Black Beans**

Preparation Time: 5 minutes
Cooking Time: 1 hour
Servings: 5

Ingredients:

- 1 small diced white onion
- 3 diced garlic cloves
- 1 lbs. cleaned & rinsed dried black beans
- 1 deseeded & diced jalapeno
- 1 teaspoon cumin
- 1 teaspoon pepper
- 2 bay leaves
- 1 teaspoon oregano
- 1 teaspoon sea salt
- 4 cups vegetable broth

Directions:

1. Add the black beans to the bowl of the instant pot,
2. Add all the ingredients.

3. Set the Instant Pot to high pressure for 35 minutes.
4. Shut the vent to seal.
5. Allow the pressure cooker to naturally release steam for about 25 minutes.
6. Taste the beans and add more salt, lime juice, and pepper to your liking.
7. As the beans cool, they will absorb the remaining liquid.
8. Before serving, remove the bay leaves.

Nutrition:

Calories: 145
Fat 0.7g
Saturated Fat 0.2g
Cholesterol: 0 mg
Sodium: 462.9 mg
Carbohydrates 26.7g
Fiber: 6.7g
Sugars: 1.8g
Protein: 8.8g

122. **Creamy Vegan Tofu Bean Tacos**

Preparation Time: 5 minutes
Cooking Time: 1 hour
Servings: 5

Ingredients:

- ½ teaspoon coriander
- ½ teaspoon cumin
- 1 garlic clove
- 1 teaspoon extra-virgin olive oil
- A pinch of sea salt
- A pinch of cayenne
- 8oz. silken tofu
- 4 soft taco shells
- 14.5 oz can vegetarian refried beans
- 1 diced tomato
- 4.0z salad greens

Directions:

1. Add beans to a small pan with a quarter cup of water.
2. Stir and cook over medium heat until the beans are warm.
3. Start making tofu cream by adding garlic to the food processor and mince it.

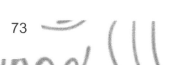

4. Next, throw in tofu to the processor, olive oil, cumin, salt, coriander and cayenne.
5. Blend to a smooth, puree-like consistency.
6. Start assembling the tacos by laying them flat on a plate.
7. Spoon beans in the center, with a few scoops of tofu cream at the side.
8. Top with tomatoes and salad greens.
9. Roll up the ends of the tacos and serve!

Nutrition:
Calories: 212
Total Fat: 5.3g
Saturated Fat: 0.7g
Cholesterol: 0 mg
Sodium: 710 mg
Carbohydrates: 30.5g
Fiber: 6g
Sugars: 1.8g
Protein: 11.3g

123. **Lentil Sloppy Joes**
Preparation Time: 10 minutes
Cooking Time: 10 minutes
Servings: 4
Ingredients:
- Whole-grain hamburger buns
- 1 tablespoon extra-virgin olive oil
- 1 medium finely chopped onion
- 1 tablespoon chili powder
- 2 15oz. cans drained & rinsed brown lentils
- 1½ cups barbecue sauce

Directions:
1. Warm the oil in a medium skillet.
2. Sauté the onion over medium heat until golden.
3. Stir together the lentils, barbecue sauce, and seasoning in the skillet.
4. Bring to a simmer by lowering the heat and let it cook for 8 minutes, or until hot.
5. Serve over cut-open hamburger buns.

Nutrition:
Calories: 211

Carbohydrates: 32g
Protein: 10g
Fat: 5g
Saturated Fat: 1g
Sodium: 320mg
Fiber: 12g
Sugar: 10g

124. **Versatile Garlic Herb Lentils**
Preparation Time: 10 minutes
Cooking Time: 20 minutes
Servings: 4
Ingredients:
- 1 tablespoon extra-virgin olive oil
- 4 minced garlic cloves
- 2 thinly sliced scallions
- Sea Salt as needed
- ½ cup finely chopped fresh parsley
- Freshly ground pepper as needed
- 2 15oz. cans drained & rinsed brown lentils
- 1 whole lemon juice

Directions:
1. Place the oil in a skillet and heat it up.
2. Sauté the garlic over low heat until golden for 2 minutes.
3. Add the lentils to the water and bring to a simmer.
4. Mash the lentils in the skillet masher to make a nice thick base.
5. Add lemon juice according to taste.
6. Mix in the scallions and sprinkle sea salt and black pepper.
7. Top with chopped parsley and serve.

Nutrition:
Calories: 300
Fat: 8g
Saturated fat: 1g
Trans fat; 0g
Carbohydrates: 49mg
Fiber 8g
Sugars 3g
Protein 18g
Sodium: 259 mg

125. Indian Style Lentil & Kidney Beans

Preparation Time: 2 minutes
Cooking Time: 10 minutes
Servings: 4

Ingredients:

- 3 sliced scallions
- 15oz. Can drained & rinsed brown lentils
- 15oz. Can drained & rinsed kidney beans
- 12oz. Indian jalfrezi sauce
- Cilantro to garnish

Directions:

1. Add all the ingredients to a saucepan.
2. Bring to a simmer.
3. Cook for 7 minutes or until hot.
4. Serve with the grains of your choice and top with cilantro.

Nutrition:

Calories 370
Carbs 37g
Protein 30g
Fat 13g
Fiber 8g
Sodium 544mg

126. Greens & Grains Healthy Bowl

Preparation Time: 5 minutes
Cooking Time: 10 minutes
Servings: 1

Ingredients:

- 3 teaspoons extra virgin olive oil
- ½ small diced red onion
- 2 minced garlic cloves
- ¼ cup chopped fresh parsley
- ½ cup leftover cooked whole grains wheat berries, spelt, barley, etc
- 1 cup cooked & dry lentils or pinto beans
- 1 cup kale
- 1 cup spinach
- 1 cup pak choy
- Sea salt as needed.
- Ground black pepper as needed

Directions:

1. In a small skillet, heat 1 teaspoon olive oil over medium heat.
2. Sauté the onion for 3 minutes, until translucent
3. Sauté the garlic for 3 minutes.
4. Add the greens and cook for 2-3 minutes until they are wilted and heated through.
5. Transfer the mixture into a bowl and season with salt and pepper.
6. In the same skillet, add 1 teaspoon of olive oil and then the leftover whole grains.
7. Sauté for a few minutes until heated through.
8. Place in the bowl with the greens and add cooked lentils
9. Serve immediately with fresh parsley.

Nutrition:

Calories: 285
Fat: 9g
Saturated Fat: 1g
Sodium: 92mg
Carbohydrates: 42g
Fiber: 10g
Sugar: 3g
Protein: 10g

127. Vegan Fulfilling Lentil Bowl

Preparation Time: 15 minutes
Cooking Time: 30 minutes
Servings: 10

Ingredients:

- 3 tablespoons extra-virgin olive oil
- 1 sweet chopped yellow onion
- 2 chopped carrots
- A pinch of nutmeg
- 2 bay leaves
- 10 roasted chopped garlic cloves
- 14.5 oz can diced tomatoes
- ½ teaspoon dried thyme
- 1/2 teaspoon paprika
- 1/2 teaspoon cumin
- 16oz. cleaned & rinsed brown lentils
- 1 tablespoon tomato paste
- 1 teaspoon dried oregano

- 2 stalks chopped celery
- 2 tablespoons red wine vinegar
- Fresh parsley for topping
- 2 (32oz.) low-sodium vegetable broth cans
- 1 teaspoon sea salt
- 1 teaspoon ground pepper

Directions:
1. In a large soup pot, heat the oil over medium-high heat.
2. Put onion, carrots and celery in the pot.
3. Stir for 8-10 minutes or until onions are limp and translucent.
4. Add salt and pepper while cooking.
5. Add roasted garlic, lentils, broth, diced tomatoes, tomato paste, and all the herbs.
6. Bring to a boil, lower heat, cover, and simmer for at least an hour, or until lentils are cooked and stir frequently.
7. Remove the bay leaves, add vinegar, taste, and adjust the seasoning if necessary.
8. Serve soup in bowls and top with parsley.

Nutrition:
Calories: 259
Carbohydrates: 29g
Protein: 13g
Fat: 9g
Saturated Fat: 1g
Sodium: 738 mg
Fiber: 12g
Sugar: 8g

128. Barley With Chickpeas & Pears
Preparation Time: 5 minutes
Cooking Time: 5 minutes
Servings: 4
Ingredients:
- ⅓ cup walnuts
- ¾ cup cashew cheese
- ¼ cup chopped parsley
- 1 cup uncooked barley

- 1 cup cooked chickpeas
- 2 chopped pears
- ⅓ cup chopped sun dried tomatoes
- 1 handful baby arugula
- 1 teaspoon dijon mustard
- 1 teaspoon dried oregano
- 3 tablespoons red onion
- ¼ cup apple cider vinegar
- ⅓ cup extra-virgin olive oil
- 2 teaspoons maple syrup
- ½ teaspoon sea salt
- ¼ teaspoon pepper

Directions:
1. Follow the package instructions for cooking barley. Drain well.
2. In a small skillet, toast the walnuts.
3. This should only take a few minutes. Allow to cool.
4. To make the dressing, add the minced onion and vinegar to a small bowl.
5. Let it marinate while you prepare the salad.
6. Divide the pears in half for garnishing and the other half for decorating salad.
7. In a large bowl, combine cooked barley, chickpeas, sun-dried tomatoes, walnuts, arugula, parsley, pears, and cashew cheese.
8. Whisk oil, maple syrup, mustard, salt, oregano, and pepper into the bowl of vinegar and red onion.
9. Toss salad mixture with dressing to coat.
10. Adjust seasoning with salt and pepper, if necessary and serve.

Nutrition:
Calories: 449
Carbohydrates: 45g
Protein: 10g
Fat: 28g
Saturated Fat: 3g
Sodium: 489 mg
Fiber: 9g
Sugar: 16g

Chapter 10: Snacks & Appetizers

129. Roasted Vegetables With Granola

Preparation Time: 15 minutes
Cooking Time: 35 minutes
Servings: 6

Ingredients:
- Extra-virgin olive oil
- 3 tablespoons balsamic vinegar
- 1 pound sliced beets
- 3 sliced carrots
- 1 sliced turnip
- 2 sliced zucchinis
- ½ chopped red onion
- Sea salt & pepper as needed
- ½ bunch Italian flat-leaf parsley
- 1 cup almonds, pecans & cashews granola

Directions:
1. Heat the oven to 450° degrees Fahrenheit.
2. Put all the vegetables in a bowl.
3. Drizzle the vegetables with olive oil.
4. Mix vinegar, sea salt, and pepper.
5. Wash parsley and chop.
6. Put chopped parsley and granola to the vegetables and mix again.
7. Grease a roasting pan with the olive oil.
8. Transfer the vegetable mixture to the roasting pan.
9. Bake for 35 minutes.
10. Take out of the oven and serve.

Nutrition:
Calories: 150.1
Fat: 4.3g
Saturated fat: 0.4g
Carbohydrates: 23.7g
Sugar: 10.5g
Fiber: 4.2g
Protein: 4.9g
Cholesterol: 0 mg

130. Roasted Sweet Potatoes with Granola

Preparation Time: 8 minutes
Cooking Time: 30 minutes
Servings: 4

Ingredients:
- ½ cup Cashew nuts & White Peach granola
- 1 ½ pounds peeled, washed & sliced in rounds sweet potatoes
- Extra-virgin Olive oil
- Salt & pepper as needed

Directions:
1. Heat oven to 425° degrees Fahrenheit.
2. Drizzle sweet potatoes with olive oil and sprinkle with salt and pepper.
3. Grease a roasting pan with olive oil.
4. Transfer potatoes to the roasting pan and fill with granola.
5. Bake for 30 minutes.
6. Take out of the oven and serve.

Nutrition:
Calories: 211.2
Fat: 2.1
Saturated fat: 0
Carbohydrates: 43.7
Sugar: 10
Fiber: 6.1
Protein: 4.7

131. Bell Peppers With Spinach & Tofu

Preparation Time: 10 minutes
Cooking Time: 35 minutes
Servings: 4

Ingredients:
- 2 tablespoons extra-virgin olive oil
- 1 chopped onion
- 2 minced garlic cloves
- 14oz. crumbled block of tofu.
- 5oz. packaged baby spinach
- 2 teaspoons Italian seasoning
- Sea Salt as needed
- Black pepper as needed
- 4 large with the top removed bell peppers

Directions:
1. Heat oven to 450 F.

2. Heat the oil in a skillet over medium flame.
3. Sauté onion and garlic for 3 minutes.
4. Place tofu and spinach and cook for 3 minutes until the spinach softens.
5. Mix in Italian seasoning, sea salt, and pepper.
6. Fill bell peppers with the mixture and transfer neatly to a greased baking sheet.
7. Bake for 25 minutes.
8. Serve immediately!

Nutrition:
Calories: 291.0
Fat: 11.4 g
Saturated Fat: 1.7 g
Cholesterol: 0.0 mg
Sodium: 138.6 mg
Potassium: 998.0 mg
Carbohydrates: 34.0 g
Fiber: 11.1 g
Sugars: 3.1 g
Protein: 19.7g

132. Coconut parsley wraps
Preparation Time: 30 minutes
Cooking Time: 60 minutes
Servings: 8
Ingredients:
- ½ cup chopped fresh parsley
- 2 tablespoons ground flaxseed
- 2 tablespoons water
- 2 whole-wheat wraps
- 1 cup sprouts
- 1 minced garlic clove
- 2 tablespoons ground hazelnuts
- 2 tablespoons flaked coconut
- 1 tablespoon coconut oil
- 1 teaspoon cayenne pepper
- Sea Salt as needed
- Black pepper as needed
- 1 lemon juice & zest

Directions:
1. Blend or process all the ingredients except the wraps in a food processor.
2. Distribute the mixture between the wraps and wrap them into rolls.

3. Chill in the fridge for 30 minutes prior to serving.

Nutrition:
Calories 209
Fat 13g
Carbohydrates 20g
Fiber 6g
Sugar 3g
Protein 6g

133. Tarragon Potato Chips
Preparation Time: 20 minutes
Cooking Time: 40 minutes
Servings: 4
Ingredients:
- 1 pound peeled & sliced potatoes
- 1 tsp smoked paprika
- ½ teaspoon garlic powder
- 1 tablespoon tarragon
- ⅛ teaspoon ground mustard
- 1 teaspoon canola oil
- ⅛ teaspoon liquid smoke
- ¼ teaspoon onion powder
- ¼ teaspoon chili powder

Directions:
1. Heat oven to 390 F.
2. Mix paprika, garlic powder, tarragon, onion powder, chili powder, salt, and mustard in a bowl.
3. Add potatoes, canola oil, liquid smoke and tarragon mixture in a separate bowl; toss to combine.
4. Transfer the potatoes to a baking tray lined with parchment paper.
5. Bake for 30 minutes.
6. Flip the potatoes after 15 minutes and cook until golden.
7. Serve immediately!

Nutrition:
Calories: 92
Fat: 4g
Saturated Fat: 1g
Cholesterol: 0 mg
Sodium: 36 mg
Carbohydrates: 13g
Fiber: 2g
Sugar: 3g
Protein: 1g

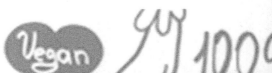

134. Tangy Ginger Avocados

Preparation Time: 5 minutes
Cooking Time: 10 minutes
Servings: 4

Ingredients:

1. 1 pressed garlic clove
2. 1 teaspoon peeled & minced fresh ginger
3. 2 pitted & halved avocados
4. Sea salt as needed
5. Ground black pepper as needed
6. 2 tablespoons balsamic vinegar
7. 4 tablespoons extra-virgin olive oil

Directions:

- Put the avocado on a platter.
- Whisk garlic, ginger, vinegar, olive oil, salt and black pepper in a bowl.
- Distribute the dressing between the avocado halves.
- Serve and enjoy!

Nutrition:
Calories: 295
Fat: 28.2g
Carbohydrates: 11.3g
Protein: 2.3g

135. Seitan Bell Pepper Balls

Preparation Time: 10 minutes
Cooking Time: 25 Minutes
Servings: 4

Ingredients:

- 1 tablespoon almond flour
- 1 teaspoon garlic powder
- 1 teaspoon onion powder
- 1 teaspoon tofu mayonnaise
- Extra-virgin Olive oil for brushing
- 1 tablespoon flax seed powder
- 3 tablespoons water
- 1 lbs. crumbled seitan
- ¼ cup chopped mixed bell peppers
- Sea salt as needed
- Black pepper as needed

Directions:

1. Line a baking sheet with parchment paper and preheat the oven to 400 F.
2. Mix the flax seed powder with water in a medium bowl and allow to thicken for 5 minutes.
3. In a large bowl, combine all the ingredients except olive oil.
4. Mix well and roll into 1-inch balls.
5. Place on the baking sheet.
6. Baste with olive oil and bake until brown for 15 to 20 minutes
7. Take out of the oven and serve.

Nutrition:
Calories: 193
Fat: 11.6g
Saturated Fat: 1.8g
Cholesterol: 0 mg
Sodium: 207.4mg
Carbohydrate: 15.3g
Fiber: 5.2g
Sugars: 6g
Protein: 8.7g

136: Avocado Toast With Flaxseeds

Preparation Time: 1 minute
Cooking Time: 2 minutes
Servings: 3

Ingredients:

- 3 slices of whole grain bread
- 1 large ripe avocado
- 1 tablespoon sesame seeds
- 1 tablespoon lemon juice
- ¼ cup chopped parsley
- 1 tablespoon flax seeds

Directions:

1. Toast the bread first.
2. Take out the avocado seeds.
3. Slice half an avocado and mash half an avocado with a fork.
4. Spread mashed avocado on 2 slices of toasted bread.
5. Sprinkle flax seeds and sesame seeds on top.
6. Top with lemon juice and chopped parsley.
7. Serve and enjoy!

Nutrition:
Protein: 31
Fat: 124g
Carbohydrates: 98g

137. Cucumber Stuffed Tomatoes

Preparation Time: 10 minutes
Cooking Time: 15 minutes
Servings: 6

Ingredients:
- 6 whole tomatoes
- 2 chopped cucumbers
- 1 lemon juice
- ½ minced red bell pepper
- 2 finely minced green onions
- 1 tablespoon minced fresh tarragon

Directions:
1. Remove the tomato tops.
2. Scoop out the seeds and pulp with a tablespoon.
3. Place them on a platter.
4. In a bowl, combine the cucumbers, lemon juice, bell pepper, scallions, tarragon, and salt.
5. Stir well to combine.
6. Assemble the tomatoes and divide the mixture among them.
7. Serve immediately!

Nutrition:
Calories: 25
Fat 25
Saturated fat: 1g
Cholesterol: 4mg
Sodium: 18 mg
Carbohydrates: 1g
Sugars: 1g
Fiber: 0g
Protein: 0g

138. Chipotle Sweet Potato Fries

Preparation Time: 20 minutes
Cooking Time: 45 minutes
Servings: 4

Ingredients:
- 4 peeled & cut into sticks medium sweet potatoes
- 2 tablespoons peanut oil
- Sea salt as needed
- 1 teaspoon chipotle pepper powder
- ¼ teaspoon ground allspice
- Ground black pepper as needed
- 1 teaspoon brown sugar
- 1 teaspoon dried rosemary

Directions:
- Combine the sweet potato fries with the remaining ingredients.
- You should bake the fries at 375 degrees F for about 45 minutes or until they are browned.
- Stir the fries a couple of times.
- You can serve these with your favorite dipping sauce.

Nutrition:
Calories: 186
Fat: 7.1g
Carbs: 29.6
Protein: 2.5g

Mushrooms

Preparation Time: 20 minutes
Cooking Time: 25 minutes
Servings: 7

Ingredients:
- 8oz. crumbled tempeh
- 1 tablespoon tahini
- 2 tablespoons soy sauce
- 1 teaspoon agave syrup
- 2 tablespoons chopped fresh cilantro
- 1 tablespoon chopped fresh mint
- 1 tablespoon rice vinegar
- 1 teaspoon smoked paprika
- ½ cup breadcrumbs
- 1 tablespoon sesame oil
- 20 portobello mushrooms

Directions:
1. Mix together the tempeh, tahini, agave syrup, vinegar, paprika, cilantro, mint, and tahini.
2. Assemble your mushrooms and divide the mixture between them.
3. Put breadcrumbs on top.
4. Brush the sesame oil over the mushrooms.
5. Preheat the oven to 400 degrees F and bake the mushrooms for 20 minutes, until they become tender and fully cooked.
6. Serve and enjoy!

Nutrition:
Calories: 133

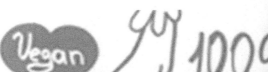

Fat: 7.8g
Carbs: 8.8g
Protein: 8.6g

140. Stuffed Bell Peppers
Preparation Time: 10 minutes
Cooking Time: 25 Minutes
Servings: 4
Ingredients:
- 1 cup bell peppers
- 1oz. chopped small tofu
- 1 cup cashew cream cheese
- 2 tablespoons melted plant butter
- 1 cup grated plant-based parmesan
- 1 tablespoon mild chili paste
- Cooking spray

Directions:
- Set the oven to 400°F.
- Cut the bell peppers in half (lengthwise) and remove the core.
- Mix tofu, cashew cream cheese, chili paste, and melted butter in a bowl.
- Fill the bell peppers with the cheese mixture and use the back of the spoon to level the filling.
- Arrange the stuffed peppers on a baking sheet greased with cooking spray.
- Top the peppers with the plant-based parmesan cheese and bake for 15-20 minutes, until the peppers have turned golden-brown and the cheese has melted.
- Place on a serving platter and serve warm.

Nutrition:
Calories 323
Fat 22g
Saturated fat 8g
Cholesterol 50 mg
Sodium 287 mg
Carbohydrates 18g
Sugars 6g
Fiber 3g
Protein 17g

141. Cauliflower With Tahini
Preparation Time: 20 minutes
Cooking Time: 40 Minutes
Servings: 5
Ingredients:
- 1/2 cup all-purpose flour
- 1/2 cup cornstarch
- 2 tablespoons tahini
- 1/2 teaspoon baking powder
- Sea salt as needed
- Ground black pepper as needed
- 2 tablespoons soy sauce
- 1 teaspoon onion powder
- 1 teaspoon garlic powder
- ½ cup vodka
- 2 tablespoons sesame oil
- 1 teaspoon cayenne pepper
- 1 teaspoon red pepper flakes
- 1 lbs. cauliflower florets

Directions:
1. Prepare your oven by preheating it to 420 degrees Fahrenheit.
2. Line a baking pan with parchment paper.
3. Combine all the ingredients except the cauliflower in a mixing bowl.
4. Brush sesame oil over the cauliflower florets.
5. Put the cauliflower florets in the prepared baking pan in a single layer.
6. Bake the cauliflower for 20 minutes.
7. Dip the cauliflower florets in the batter and bake for a further 20 minutes.
8. Serve hot.

Nutrition:
Calories: 247
Fat: 11.9g
Carbohydrates: 31.4g
Protein: 5.2g

142. Mexican-style Onion Rings
Preparation Time: 10 minutes
Cooking Time: 35 minutes
Servings: 6
Ingredients:
- 2 cut into rings medium onions
- ¼ cup all-purpose flour

- ¼ cup spelt flour
- ⅓ cup unsweetened rice milk
- ½ cup ale beer
- Sea salt as needed
- Ground black pepper as needed
- ½ teaspoon cayenne pepper
- 1 tablespoon extra-virgin olive oil
- ½ teaspoon mustard seeds
- 1 cup crushed tortilla chips

Directions:
1. Prepare your oven by preheating it to 420 degrees Fahrenheit.
2. Mix milk, flour, and beer together in a large bowl.
3. Mix the spices in another large bowl with crushed tortilla chips.
4. Dip the onion rings in the flour mixture.
5. Roll them over the spiced mixture, pressing down to make sure they are well coated.
6. Place the onion rings on a parchment-lined baking sheet.
7. Bake for approximately 30 minutes after brushing them with olive oil.
8. Take it out once golden and crispy.
9. Serve hot with your favorite dip.

Nutrition:
Calories: 213

Fat: 10.6g
Carbs: 26.2g
Protein: 4.3g

143. Carrot Energy Balls
Preparation Time: 10 minutes
Cooking Time: 10 minutes
Servings: 8
Ingredients:
- 1 large grated carrot
- 1 ½ cups old-fashioned oats
- 1 cup pitied dates
- 1 cup raisins
- 1 cup coconut flakes
- ¼ teaspoon ground cloves
- ½ teaspoon ground cinnamon

Directions:
1. Put all ingredients in your food processor and pulse until they are combined into a sticky, uniform mixture.
2. Make equal sized balls from the batter.
3. Refrigerate until you are ready to serve.

Nutrition:
Calories: 495
Fat: 21.1g
Carbs: 58.4g
Protein: 22.1g

Chapter 11: Sides

144. Lemonish Steamed Green Beans
Preparation Time: 5 minutes
Cooking Time: 5 minutes
Servings: 4
Ingredients:
- 1oz. fresh trimmed green beans
- 1 tablespoon fresh lemon juice & zest
- 1 tablespoon extra-virgin olive oil
- ½ teaspoon kosher salt
- Fresh ground black pepper
- 1 ⅓ cups water

Directions:
1. Add 1 ½ cups of water into a pot.
2. Once it starts boiling, put in green beans.
3. Cover and give steam for 4-5 minutes or until fork tender.
4. Drain the water and add the beans to a mixture of olive oil, lemon juice, zest, salt and a generous sprinkling of black pepper.
5. Serve along with your favorite dishes.

Nutrition:
Calories: 67
Fat 3.8g
Saturated Fat 0.6g
Carbohydrates 8.5g
Fiber 3.2g
Sugars 3.8g

145. Steamed Broccoli
Preparation Time: 5 minutes
Cooking Time: 5 minutes
Servings: 4
Ingredients:
- 2 large heads broccoli
- ¼ cup thinly sliced green onions
- 2 tablespoons extra-virgin olive oil
- ½ teaspoon kosher salt
- Freshly ground black pepper as needed
- 1 ½ cup water

Directions:
1. Cut broccoli into florets.
2. Add 1 ½ cup water into a saucepan.
3. Once it starts boiling, put in the florets.
4. Cover and give steam for 4-5 minutes or until fork tender.
5. Drain the water and add the broccoli to a mixture of olive oil, salt, onion and a generous sprinkling of ground black pepper.
6. Serve along with your favorite dishes.
7. Carefully remove the broccoli to a bowl. Toss with the olive oil, kosher salt, and drained red onions.
8. Top with freshly ground black pepper.

Nutrition:
Calories: 147
Total Fat: 9.6g
Saturated Fat: 2.5g
Carbohydrate: 12.6g
Fiber: 4.6g
Sugar: 3.7g
Proteins 6.2g

146. Best Sauteed Kale
Preparation Time: 5 minutes
Cooking Time: 3 minutes
Servings: 4
Ingredients:
- 2 bunches Tuscan kale
- 2 garlic cloves
- 2 tablespoons extra-virgin olive oil
- ¼ teaspoon kosher salt
- Fresh ground pepper
- Lemon wedges

Directions:
1. Wash and dry the kale leaves.
2. De-stem and roughly chop.
3. Peel and mince the garlic cloves.
4. Pour olive oil to a large skillet over medium-high heat.

5. Once hot, add minced garlic and kale, cook for 3 minutes.
6. Stir often until droopy and turn bright green in color.
7. Take off from heat and sprinkle kosher salt and fresh ground pepper.
8. Discard the garlic cloves and serve with your favorite dishes and lemon wedges

Nutrition:
Calories: 118
Fat: 8.1g
Saturated Fat: 1.1g
Carbohydrates: 10.4g
Fiber: 4.1g
Sugars: 2.6g

147. Peas with Lemon
Preparation Time: 2 minutes
Cooking Time: 3 minutes
Servings: 1
Ingredients:
- 2 cups frozen peas
- 2 garlic cloves
- 1 tablespoon nutritional yeast
- 1 tablespoon olive oil
- ¼ teaspoon sea salt
- Fresh ground pepper as needed
- ½ lemon zest

Directions:
1. Rinse peas under warm running water and drain.
2. Peel and mince garlic cloves.
3. Add nutritional yeast and olive oil to a large skillet and place over medium heat.
4. Sauté in minced garlic and peas, cooking for 2 minutes until completely warm but still vivid in color.
5. Sprinkle black pepper, sea salt, and lemon zest
6. Remove the garlic cloves from the peas before serving.
7. It is a healthy side dish to have with a variety of grains.

Nutrition:
Calories: 107
Fat: 6.6g
Saturated Fat: 2.4g
Carbohydrates: 9.1g
Fiber: 3g
Sugars: 3.4g

148. Smashed Brussels Sprouts
Preparation Time: 10 minutes
Cooking Time: 30 minutes
Servings: 1
Ingredients:
- 1 ½ oz. stemless Brussels sprouts
- 3 tablespoons extra-virgin olive oil
- 1 tablespoon sea salt
- ⅓ cup cashew cheese
- ¼ teaspoon garlic powder
- ¼ teaspoon onion powder
- Ground black pepper as needed

Directions:
1. Set the oven to 450 degrees Fahrenheit.
2. Bring a pot of water to boil after adding 1 tablespoon of sea salt to it.
3. Cut off the rough ends of the Brussels sprouts and boil them for 8 minutes, until tender yet vivid in color.
4. Drain the water and let them steam in a colander for some time.
5. Dry them with a clean kitchen towel and transfer to a large bowl.
6. Add olive oil, sea salt, onion, garlic and black pepper powder to the bowl.
7. Toss to combine well.
8. Transfer the sprouts to a parchment-lined baking tray.
9. Smash them slightly with a small skillet until they are a little mashed, but not overly mushy.
10. Top with some cashew cheese and bake for 25 minutes, or until nicely brown and crispy.
11. Remove from the oven once baked and season with salt if necessary.

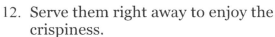

12. Serve them right away to enjoy the crispiness.

Nutrition:
Calories: 154
Fat: 8g
Cholesterol: 2mg
Sodium: 248 mg
Carbohydrates: 16g
Fiber 7g
Protein 7g
Sugars 4g

149. **Quick Baked Potatoes**
Preparation Time: 5 minutes
Cooking Time: 30 minutes
Servings: 1
Ingredients:
- 4 medium russet potatoes
- Extra-virgin olive oil as needed
- Sea Salt & pepper to taste

Directions:
1. Set the oven to 450 degrees Fahrenheit.
2. Slice the potatoes in half after washing them.
3. Prepare a baking sheet with parchment paper.
4. Apply enough olive oil to coat the potatoes and place them on the baking sheet.
5. Sprinkle sea salt over them.
6. Fork prick the potatoes several times on top, cut side down.
7. Bake for 25 to 35 minutes, depending on the size of the potatoes, until the potatoes are tender and lightly browned from around the edges.
8. To check if they are done, prick them with a fork.
9. If necessary, add another sprinkle of salt.
10. Serve as a side dish with any meal.

Nutrition:
Calories:168
Fat: 0.2g
Saturated Fat 0.1g

Carbohydrates 38.5g
Fiber 2.8g
Sugars 1.3g

150. **Crispy Breaded Cauliflower**
Preparation Time: 10 minutes
Cooking Time: 30 minutes
Servings: 4
Ingredients:
- 1 medium head chopped cauliflower florets
- ½ cup gluten-free breadcrumbs
- ½ cup cornmeal
- 1 tablespoon peanut butter
- 1 tablespoon maple syrup
- 1 teaspoon cumin
- 1 teaspoon garlic powder
- ¼ teaspoon turmeric
- ½ teaspoon sea salt
- 1 tablespoon refined coconut oil
- 1 teaspoon smoked paprika
- 2 tablespoons tamari
- ½ tablespoon hot sauce

Directions:
1. Preheat the oven to 400F.
2. Place cauliflower florets in a large bowl.
3. Mix the dry ingredients in a small bowl.
4. Place a saucepan over medium flame and whisk in all the wet ingredients for 2 minutes, or until well-combined and slightly darkened.
5. Stir in the sauce to the cauliflower bowl and make sure the florets are evenly coated.
6. Take half of the dry mixture and add to the bowl of cauliflower and mix well.
7. Add the remaining dry mixture to ensure each floret is covered properly.
8. Use your hands to transfer the breaded cauliflower florets onto a parchment lined baking sheet.
9. Put in the oven for 30 minutes and do not forget to flip after 15 minutes.

10. Remove from oven when done and serve immediately with your favorite dip.

Nutrition:
Calories: 151
Fat: 6.4g
Saturated Fat: 3.5g
Carbohydrates: 20.9g
Fiber: 4g
Sugars: 7.1g

151. "Delicata" Squash Tahini Fries
Preparation Time: 5 minutes
Cooking Time: 25 minutes
Servings: 4
Ingredients:
- 4 "delicata" squash
- Extra-virgin olive oil as needed
- ½ teaspoon kosher salt
- 2 garlic cloves
- ¼ cup lemon tahini sauce
- Black pepper as needed
- 2 tablespoons vegan butter

Directions:
1. Heat the oven to 450°F.
2. Wash, cut in half lengthwise, and scoop out the seeds of the squash.
3. Slice each half into 1/2-inch pieces.
4. Drizzle olive oil over the slices and place in a bowl.
5. Stir in kosher salt and freshly ground black pepper as needed.
6. Place the squash in a single layer on a baking sheet covered with parchment paper.
7. Bake for about 25 minutes until tender and nicely browned.
8. Start preparing the buffalo sauce.
9. Start by melting the butter in a saucepan and mince the garlic.
10. Stir tahini sauce into butter and garlic.
11. Serve breaded squash fresh out of the oven with buffalo sauce.

Nutrition:
Calories: 74
Fat: 3.6g
Saturated Fat: 0.3g

Cholesterol: 0 mg
Sodium: 584.6mg
Carbohydrates: 11.2g
Fiber: 1.6g
Sugars: 0g
Protein: 0.9g

152. Quick & Easy Cilantro Lime Rice
Preparation Time: 10 minutes
Cooking Time: 15 minutes
Servings: 4
Ingredients:
- 1 cup long-grain brown rice
- ½ teaspoon kosher salt
- 1 tablespoon coconut oil
- 2 tablespoons lime juice
- ½ teaspoon garlic powder
- ¼ cup finely chopped cilantro
- 1 teaspoon lime zest

Directions:
1. Add 2 cups of water to a saucepan and add your rice.
2. Bring the water to a boil, cover and allow it to simmer until the water has completely vanished.
3. Mix lime juice, zest and cilantro in a small bowl.
4. Remove the cover from the rice and add salt and garlic powder.
5. Put the cover back and let it steam for 10 minutes.
6. Uncover and mix in the coconut oil and the cilantro mix from the small bowl.
7. Serve it immediately with any meal .

Nutrition:
Calories: 271
Fat: 0.4g
Saturated Fat: 0.1g
Trans Fat: 0g
Cholesterol: 0mg
Sodium: 787mg
Potassium: 82mg
Carbohydrates: 60g
Fiber: 0.3g
Sugars: 0.3g
Protein: 5g

153. **Simple Homemade Marinara Sauce**

Preparation Time: 10 minutes
Cooking Time: 20 minutes
Servings: 4

Ingredients:
- 1 yellow chopped onion
- 1 tablespoon extra-virgin olive oil
- 3 minced garlic cloves
- 1 teaspoon dried basil
- 1 teaspoon dried oregano
- ½ teaspoon ground black pepper
- Sea salt as needed
- 28oz. whole San Marzano tomatoes

Directions:
1. Heat olive oil in a saucepan over a medium flame.
2. Sauté onion and garlic until translucent.
3. Stir in the juicy tomatoes, oregano, basil, salt and mix well.
4. Mash up the tomatoes with a potato masher in the saucepan.
5. Continue cooking the sauce until it simmers.
6. Then, turn the flame to a simmer for 20 minutes and cover. Stir frequently !
7. Serve the marinara chunky or puree it with a hand blender for a smoother consistency.

Nutrition:
Calories: 55
Fat: 4g
Carbohydrates: 4g
Fiber: 2g
Sugar: 1g
Protein: 1g

154. **A Classic Hummus Recipe**

Preparation Time: 17 minutes
Cooking Time: 1 hour
Servings: 4

Ingredients:
- 1 cup dry chickpeas
- 2 teaspoons baking soda
- 1 teaspoon fine sea salt
- 1 teaspoon ground cumin
- 1 cup tahini
- ½ cup lemon juice
- 2 garlic cloves
- 4-6 tablespoons ice-cold water
- 1 tablespoon extra-virgin olive oil

Directions:
1. Soak chickpeas in a large bowl with 1 teaspoon of baking soda and plenty of water as they will expand in size.
2. Keep them soaked for 12 hours or overnight at room temperature.
3. Drain the water and rinse under cold water.
4. Cook the chickpeas in a medium pan with another 1 teaspoon baking powder added with enough water.
5. Let it boil over high heat and remove any film that covers the surface.
6. Lower the flame to low-medium, sprinkle some salt, and allow it to simmer half covered, until fully cooked and it starts to crumble.
7. Chickpeas can easily take 1-2 hours to cook. You only need to keep them filled with water. Meanwhile, start preparing the tahini sauce.
8. Combine garlic, lemon juice, cumin and salt in a fast blender and blend until smooth.
9. After a rest of 10 minutes, add tahini and give it a blend until you reach a creamy consistency.
10. Gradually add water, 2 tablespoons at a time to thin out the sauce.
11. It will turn lighter and creamier.
12. Drain the chickpeas and add to the sauce and blend until smooth.
13. Do not forget to scrape the sides.
14. As the blender runs, drizzle in olive oil to create a lightweight texture.
15. Place the hummus into a wide bowl and use the back of the spoon to flatten it.
16. Serve it with crackers.

Nutrition:
Calories: 292
Fat: 19g
Carbohydrates: 23g

Fiber: 7g
Sugar: 2g
Protein: 10g

155. Vegan Cheesy Queso Dip

Preparation Time: 5 minutes
Cooking Time: 20 minutes
Servings: 3

Ingredients:

- 1 cup raw cashews
- 1 cup cubed butternut squash
- 1 cup unsweetened plant-based milk
- 1 tablespoon nutritional yeast
- 1 seeded & quartered orange bell pepper
- 2 cups &1 teaspoon water
- ½ teaspoon salt
- ¼ teaspoon smoked paprika
- 1 teaspoon tapioca flour
- ½ teaspoon onion powder
- ½ teaspoon garlic powder

Directions:

1. Combine squash, cashews, bell pepper and 2 cups of water in a medium pan.
2. Bring to a boil and reduce the heat to medium.
3. Cook until the squash and cashews turn soft.
4. Once done, drain and add to a blender.
5. Put in nutritional yeast, plant-based milk, onion powder, smoked paprika, and garlic powder.
6. Blend until creamy and smooth.
7. Return the squash mixture back to the saucepan and slowly allow it to boil over medium heat.
8. Mix often and cook for 3 minutes.
9. In a separate bowl, combine tapioca flour and 1 teaspoon of water to create a slurry.
10. Transfer the slurry to the squash sauce and cook, while stirring steadily, until the sauce turns thick and creamy.

Nutrition:
Calories: 85
Fat: 6g
Carbohydrates: 7g
Protein: 3g
Fiber: 1g
Sodium: 109mg

Chapter 11: Sauces & Condiments

156. Creamy Coconut butter
Preparation Time: 1 minute
Cooking Time: 1 minute
Servings: 16 tablespoons
Ingredients:
- 4 cups desiccated coconut

Directions:
1. Blend the coconut in a blender on high for a minute, or until creamy.
2. The end product will be creamy but slightly grainy, which is natural.
3. Store it in an airtight container in the fridge for 3 months or six months in the freezer.

Nutrition:
Calories: 140
Fat: 14g
Carbohydrates: 5g
Fiber: 3g
Sugar: 2g
Protein: 1g

157. Quick Almond Butter
Preparation Time: 1 minute
Cooking Time: 12 minutes
Servings: 32 tablespoons
Ingredients:
- 4 cups organic almonds

Directions:
1. Preheat the oven at 325 Fahrenheit.
2. Spread the almonds on a baking sheet in a single layer and roast for 10-12 minutes.
3. Keep checking as they can roast too quickly.
4. They will be fragrant and crispy once done.
5. Blend them on high in a blender until creamy and smooth.
6. Add any tasteless oil if the almonds are too dry.
7. Keep them in an air-tight container in the refrigerator for 1 month.

Nutrition:
Calories: 98
Fat: 9g
Trans Fat: 1g
Carbohydrates: 4g
Fiber: 2g
Protein: 4g

158. Quick Cheese Sauce
Preparation Time: 5 minutes
Cooking Time: 25 minutes
Servings: 6
Ingredients:
- A pinch of salt
- A pinch of ground black pepper
- ½ cup nutritional yeast
- ⅓ cup extra-virgin olive oil
- ½ cup water
- ½ teaspoon of onion powder
- ½ teaspoon of garlic powder
- 1 tablespoon freshly squeezed lemon juice
- 1 cup washed, peeled & diced carrots
- 2 cups washed, peeled & diced potatoes

Directions:
1. In a saucepan over medium flame, boil the carrots and potatoes until soft.
2. Drain and put in the blender.
3. Add the rest of the ingredients to the blender and blend until smooth.
4. Serve hot with crackers.
5. Seal in air-tight jar and store in the refrigerator for up to four days or freeze it for longer life.

Nutrition:
Calories: 110
Fat: 8.4g
Saturated Fat: 3.8g
Cholesterol: 18mg
Sodium: 522mg
Potassium: 19mg
Carbohydrates: 4.3g
Fiber: 0.3g
Sugars: 0.3g
Protein: 4.2g

159. Raspberry Chia Pudding

Preparation Time: 2 minutes
Cooking Time: 0 Minute
Servings: 2

Ingredients:
- 4 tablespoons chia seeds
- 1 cup coconut milk
- ½ cup raspberries

Directions:
1. Blend raspberry and coconut milk in a blender until smooth.
2. Fill Mason jar with mixture.
3. Add chia seeds to a jar and stir well.
4. Close the lid tightly and shake well.
5. Refrigerate for 3 hours before serving.

Nutrition:
Calories: 312
Fat: 20.4g
Saturated fat: 5g
Sodium: 45.6mg
Potassium: 762.9mg
Carbohydrates: 24.4g
Sugar: 2.7g
Fiber: 20g

160. Homemade Ketchup

Preparation Time: 10 minutes
Cooking Time: 30 Minutes
Servings: 12

Ingredients:
- ⅛ teaspoon mustard powder
- ⅛ teaspoon ground cloves
- ¼ teaspoon paprika
- 3 tablespoons apple cider vinegar
- ¼ cup powdered monk fruit
- 1 cup water
- 6oz. tomato paste
- ½ teaspoon garlic powder
- ¾ teaspoon onion powder
- 1 teaspoon sea salt

Directions:
1. Whisk together all the ingredients in a small saucepan.
2. Bring the pan to a simmer for 30 minutes on low heat.
3. Put the lid on and do not forget to stir frequently

4. Once thickened, blend it in a smooth and puree-like consistency.

Nutrition:
Calories: 20
Total Fat: 0g
Saturated Fat: 0g
Cholesterol: 0 mg
Sodium: 10 mg
Carbohydrates: 5g
Fiber: 1g
Sugar: 1g
Protein: 1g

161. Whipped Cream

Preparation Time: 2 minutes
Cooking Time: 0 minutes
Servings: 2

Ingredients:
- ¼ cup powdered sugar
- 1 teaspoon unsweetened vanilla extract
- 14oz. unsweetened & chilled coconut milk

Directions:
1. Leave an empty bowl in the freezer overnight.
2. Separate coconut milk from solid and transfer that coconut solid to the chilled bowl.
3. Add the rest of the ingredients and beat for 3 minutes with a beater until smooth and well-combined.
4. Serve straight away.

Nutrition:
Calories: 40.4
Fat: 1 g
Carbohydrates: 8 g
Protein: 0 g
Fiber: 0 g

162. Easy Granola

Preparation Time: 5 minutes
Cooking Time: 1 hour 30 minutes
Servings: 7

Ingredients:
- ½ cup pure maple syrup
- ¼ cup coconut oil
- ¾ teaspoon fine sea salt

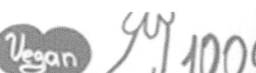

- 5 cups rolled oats
- ¾ cup unsweetened & shredded coconut
- 1 cup slivered almonds

Directions:
1. Stir all of your ingredients together in a bowl, and then preheat your oven to 250 degrees.
2. Be sure to evenly spread the granola out over two baking sheets.
3. Bake for one hour and fifteen minutes, stirring every twenty minutes.
4. Let it cool before serving.

Nutrition:
Calories: 239
Protein: 6 g
Fat: 11 g
Carbohydrates: 32 g

163. Quick Breakfast Cereal
Preparation time: 5 minutes
Cooking Time: 45 minutes
Servings: 6
Ingredients:
- ¼ tablespoon vegan butter
- 1 teaspoon cinnamon
- 1 cup raw brown rice
- ½ cup seedless raisins
- 2 ¼ cups water
- Honey as needed

Directions:
1. In a saucepan, combine your cinnamon, raisins, rice, and butter, then add your water.
2. Let it come to a boil and allow it to simmer with a lid on for 40 minutes
3. Use a fork to fluff.
4. Serve with honey

Nutrition:
Calories: 160
Protein: 3 g
Fat: 1.5 g
Carbohydrates: 34 g

164. Quick Black Bean Dip
Preparation Time: 2 minutes
Cooking Time: 10 Minutes

Servings: 2
Ingredients:
- 14 oz. drained & rinsed black beans
- 1 lemon juice & zest
- ¼ cup water
- 1 teaspoon cumin
- 1 tablespoon tamari
- ¼ cup fresh & chopped cilantro
- a pinch of cayenne pepper

Directions:
1. Blend everything except cilantro until smooth.
2. Serve with cilantro on top with crackers or chips.

Nutrition:
Calories: 190
Protein: 13 g
Fat: 1 g
Carbohydrates: 35 g

165. Simple Guacamole
Preparation Time: 2 minutes
Cooking Time: 10 minutes
Servings: 1 ½ cups
Ingredients:
- 2 peeled & pitted avocados
- ½ lemon juice
- A pinch of sea salt
- 1 chopped tomato
- 1 white & green parts chopped scallion
- 2 tablespoons chopped fresh cilantro

Directions:
1. Mash avocados, lime juice, and salt together in a medium bowl until you reach your preferred consistency.
2. Mix the cilantro, tomato, and scallion well.
3. Serve as soon as possible.

Nutrition:
Calories: 113
Fat: 10g
Carbohydrates: 7g
Protein: 2g
Fiber: 5g
Sodium: 32mg

166. Plant-Based Parmesan

Preparation Time: 2 minutes
Cooking Time: 10 minutes
Servings: 1

Ingredients:
- 1 cup raw cashews
- ½ teaspoon salt
- ½ cup nutritional yeast

Directions:
1. Process the cashews in the blender until they turn into a fine powder.
2. Put the fine cashew powder in a small bowl with nutritional yeast and salt.
3. Stir well with a spoon.
4. If you have any leftovers, place them into an airtight container and refrigerate for up to ten days or freeze for up to three months.

Nutrition:
Calories: 79
Fat: 5g
Carbohydrates: 5g
Protein: 3g
Fiber: 0g
Sodium: 195mg

167. Helpful Oat Milk

Preparation Time: 5 minutes
Cooking Time: 5 minutes
Servings: 4 cups

Ingredients:
- 1 cup rolled oats
- 3 pitted dates
- 4 cups water
- Nut milk bag/cheesecloth for straining

Directions:
1. Blend oats, water and dates in a blender on high for 45 minutes until the oats are finely ground and the liquid turns creamy.
2. Do not over-blend the ingredients or the texture will turn to a slimy consistency.
3. Strain the milk through a nut milk bag or cheesecloth to catch the unblended pieces.

4. Refrigerate it for up to four days in an airtight container.

Nutrition:
Calories: 90
Fat: 3g
Carbohydrates: 13g
Protein: 1g
Fiber: 0g
Sodium: 12mg

168. Raw Date Paste

Preparation Time: 10 minutes
Cooking Time: 10 minutes
Servings: 2 cups

Ingredients:
- 1 cup pitted & chopped Medjool dates,
- 1½ cups water

Directions:
1. Blend the dates with water in a blender until they are smooth.
2. Refrigerate up to 7 days in an airtight container.

Nutrition:
Calories: 21
Fat: 0g
Carbohydrates: 5g
Protein: 0g
Fiber: 1g
Sodium: 0mg

169. Easy Almond Nut Milk

Preparation time: 5 minutes
Cooking Time: 5 minutes
Servings: 5

Ingredients:
- 1 cup soaked overnight & drained almonds
- 4 cups water
- 3 pitted dates
- 1 teaspoon vanilla extract

Directions:
1. Put the soaked almonds, dates, vanilla, and water into a blender and blend on high for 3 to 4 minutes, until completely smooth.
2. Strain the blended mix through a nut milk bag or cheesecloth.

3. Add it to an airtight storage container and refrigerate for 4 days only.

Nutrition:
Calories: 25
Fat: 2g
Carbohydrates: 1g
Protein: 0g
Fiber: 0g
Sodium: 22mg

170. **Tomato Salsa**
Preparation Time: 10 minutes
Cooking Time: 10 minutes
Servings: 3
Ingredients:
- 4 peeled & washed tomatoes
- ½ peeled medium yellow onion
- 3 stemmed & seeded jalapenos
- 1 garlic clove
- 1 cup water
- 1 cup fresh cilantro
- ¼ teaspoon salt

Directions:
1. Blend all the ingredients in a blender until smooth.
2. You may add salt if you wish.
3. Refrigerate for up to ten days in an airtight container.

Nutrition:
Calories: 7
Fat: 0g
Carbohydrates: 1g
Protein: 0g
Fiber: 0g
Sodium: 50mg

Chapter 14: Desserts

171. Cocoa Almond Energy Bites

Preparation Time: 10 minutes
Cooking Time: 10 minutes
Servings: 12

Ingredients:
- 2 tablespoons smooth natural almond butter
- 1 ½ cups pitted "medjool" dates
- 1 cup almonds
- 3 tablespoons cocoa powder
- 1 tablespoon protein powder

Directions:
1. Process the almonds until they are coarsely ground in a food processor fitted with an S blade.
2. Do not over-process the almonds.
3. Put dates, almond butter, protein powder and cocoa powder in the food processor with the almonds, and process until well-combined.
4. The mixture must be soft and crumbly but should hold its shape when you press it.
5. Add a tablespoon or two of coconut oil if the mixture is too dry.
6. Make 1-inch/2.5-cm balls using about a tablespoon of the mixture.
7. Put on a serving platter.
8. Continue until all the mixture is used up.
9. Let the almond butter energy bites chill for 15-30 minutes before serving.

Nutrition:
Calories: 139
Fat: 8g
Carbohydrates: 17g
Fiber: 4g
Sugar: 11g
Protein: 5g

172. Quick Banana Fritters

Preparation Time: 2 minutes
Cooking Time: 20 Minutes
Servings: 8

Ingredients:
- 4 bananas
- ¼ teaspoon cinnamon Powder
- ¼ teaspoon nutmeg
- 3 tablespoons maple syrup
- 1 cup coconut flour

Directions:
1. Set the oven to 350° F.
2. Combine the bananas with all the ingredients in a large mixing bowl.
3. Make small 1-inch-thick fritters with 2 tablespoons of the mixture.
4. Grease a baking tray and place the fritters there.
5. In a preheated oven, bake fritters for about 10-15 minutes until golden brown on both sides.
6. Once baked, remove from oven and serve!

Nutrition:
Calories: 414
Fat: 20g
Saturated Fat: 1.8g
Trans Fat: 0.1g
Cholesterol: 31mg
Sodium: 255mg
Potassium; 466m
Carbohydrates: 56g
Fiber; 3.7g
Sugars; 15g
Protein; 4.5g

173. Chocolate Coconut Brownies

Preparation Time: 10 minutes
Cooking time: 35 minutes
Servings: 12

Ingredients:
- 1 cup whole-grain flour
- ½ teaspoon sea salt
- 1 cup light brown sugar
- ½ cup unsweetened cocoa powder
- 1 teaspoon baking powder
- ½ cup canola oil

- ½ cup vegan semisweet chocolate chips
- ½ cup sweetened shredded coconut
- ¾ cup unsweetened coconut milk
- 1 teaspoon pure vanilla extract
- 1 teaspoon coconut extract

Directions:
1. Set the oven to 350°F.
2. Prepare an 8-inch square baking pan by greasing it.
3. Mix flour, cocoa, baking powder, and salt together in a large bowl.
4. Mix sugar and oil together in a separate medium bowl.
5. Add coconut milk and the vanilla and mix until smooth.
6. Combine the wet and dry ingredients and mix well.
7. Lastly, fold in the chocolate chips and coconut with a spatula.
8. Pour the batter into the prepared baking pan.
9. Bake 35-40 minutes or until a toothpick inserted in the center comes out clean.
10. Once done, transfer to a cooling rack for half an hour and serve .
11. Store the leftovers in an airtight container.

Nutrition:
Calories: 200
Carbohydrates: 30g
Fat: 9g
Protein: 3g

176. Lime & Watermelon Granita
Preparation Time: 10 minutes
Cooking Time: 6 hours
Servings: 4
Ingredients:
- 2 tablespoons lemon juice
- ½ cup pure cane sugar
- 8 cups seedless watermelon chunks
- Lemon zest

Directions:
1. Combine all the ingredients except the zest in a blender or food processor and process until smooth.

2. Two batches may be required.
3. Stir both batches well after processing.
4. Fill a 9-by-1-inch glass dish with the mixture.
5. Chill for 2 or 3 hours.
6. Scrape away the top layer of ice with a fork after removing it from the freezer.
7. Let the shaved ice be on top and place it back into the freezer.
8. Do this a few more times until all the ice has been scraped
9. Serve frozen with strips of lime zest.

Nutrition:
Calories: 45
Fat: 0 g
Saturated Fat: 0 g
Carbohydrates: 12 g
Sugar: 10 g
Fiber: 0 g
Protein: 1 g
Sodium: 1mg

177. Hazelnut Topped Coconut Caramelized Bananas
Preparation Time: 5 minutes
Cooking Time: 15 minutes
Servings: 4
Ingredients:
- 2 tablespoons coconut oil
- 2 tablespoons coconut sugar
- 2 peeled and halved bananas
- 2 tablespoons spiced apple cider
- Chopped hazelnuts for serving

Directions:
1. Melt coconut oil in a skillet over medium heat.
2. Cook bananas for 2 minutes
3. Flip and cook another 2 minutes
4. Add sugar and cider and cook for 2 minutes until sugar thickens and is caramelized.
5. Serve in bowls with hazelnuts on top.

Nutrition:
Calories: 119

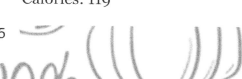

Sugar: 11.2g
Sodium: 42mg
Fat: 6g
Saturated Fat: 3.7g
Carbohydrates: 17.6g
Fiber: 1.6g
Protein: 0.7g
Cholesterol: 15mg

178. Lime Coconut Chia Pudding

Preparation Time: 10 minutes
Cooking Time: 20 Minutes
Servings: 4

Ingredients:
- 1 lemon juice & zest
- 14oz. can coconut milk
- 2 dates
- 2 tablespoons whole chia seeds

Directions:
1. Add all the ingredients to a blender and blend until smooth.
2. Let cool in the fridge for a few minutes.
3. Serve topped with coconut cream.

Nutrition:
Calories 226
Total fat: 20g
Carbs: 13g
Fiber: 5g
Protein: 3g

179. Coconut Fat Rounds

Preparation Time: 2 minutes
Cooking Time: 2 minutes
Servings: 4

Ingredients:
- 1 can unsweetened coconut flakes
- 20 drops liquid stevia
- ¾ can coconut oil
- 1 can coconut milk

Directions:
1. Melt coconut oil in the microwave for 20 seconds on low temperature.
2. Stir in milk and stevia.
3. Combine coconut flakes well and add to ice cube trays for an hour.
4. Serve once done!

Nutrition:

Calories 194
Fat 16.8g
Saturated Fat 10g
Trans Fat 0g
Cholesterol 3.2mg
Sodium 1.1mg
Potassium 89.4mg
Carbohydrates 3.5g
Fiber 1.5g
Sugar 0.3g
Protein 3.8g

180. Homemade Easy Raisins

Preparation Time: 10 minutes
Cooking Time: 6 hours

Ingredients:
- 2 bunches of seedless grapes
- A pinch of sea salt

Directions:
1. Place grapes on a parchment-lined baking sheet.
2. Season with a pinch of salt.
3. Bake in a preheated oven at 225 degrees Fahrenheit for about 6 hours or until they are dried
4. Allow to cool completely.
5. Keep in a sealed container in the refrigerator for weeks.

Nutrition:
Calories: 83
Fat: 0.1g
Carbs: 21.7g
Protein: 0.8g

181. Vanilla Mint Ice Cream

Preparation Time: 5 minutes
Cooking Time: 10 minutes
Servings: 4

Ingredients:
- 2 pitted avocados
- 1 ¼ cups coconut cream
- ½ tsp vanilla extract
- 2 tablespoons erythritol
- 2 teaspoons chopped mint leaves

Directions:
1. Put all the ingredients in a blender and blend until smooth.

2. Transfer the mixture to an ice cream maker and freezer according to the manufacturer's guidelines.
3. Once ready, serve by scooping out the ice cream into a bowl.

Nutrition:
Calories: 170
Carbohydrates: 23.g
Fiber: 1g
Protein: 10g
Fat: 5g
Cholesterol: 25mg
Sodium: 95mg

182. Peanut Chocolate Brownies
Preparation Time: 20 minutes
Cooking Time: 40 minutes
Servings: 12
Ingredients:
- 1 ¾ cups whole-grain flour
- 1 teaspoon baking powder
- ½ teaspoon sea salt
- ½ cup vegan chocolate chips
- ½ cup chopped peanuts
- ¼ cup canola oil
- 1 tablespoon ground nutmeg
- ½ teaspoon ground cinnamon
- ½ cup water
- ⅓ cup pure date sugar
- 2 teaspoons grated fresh ginger
- 3 tablespoons unsweetened cocoa powder
- ½ cup dark molasses

Directions:
1. Set the oven to 360 Fahrenheit.
2. Take a bowl and add baking powder, flour, cinnamon, nutmeg, salt, cinnamon and cocoa powder.
3. Combine chocolate chips and cocoa powder in a separate bowl.
4. In a separate bowl, combine molasses, oil, sugar, water and ginger.
5. Mix in the flour mixture.
6. Place in a greased baking pan for about 35 minutes
7. Allow it to cool before serving.

Nutrition:
Calories: 380
Total carbs: 57g
Fat: 16g
Protein: 3g

183. Classic Bread Pudding with Sultanas
Preparation Time: 20 minutes
Cooking Time: 2 Hours
Servings: 4
Ingredients:
- 10oz. cubed day-old bread
- 2 cups coconut milk
- ½ teaspoon ground cloves
- ½ teaspoon ground cinnamon
- ½ cup coconut sugar
- 1 teaspoon vanilla extract
- ½ cup Sultanas

Directions:
1. Spread the bread cubes in a thinly greased
2. baking dish.
3. Add milk, sugar, vanilla, cinnamon, cloves to a blender and blend until smooth.
4. Scoop the mixture and put it all over the bread cubes.
5. Press the cubes to ensure they are soaking up the mixture well.
6. Add in sultanas and let it aside for an hour.
7. Bake in a preheated oven at 350 degrees Fahrenheit, or until the surface looks golden-brown.
8. Allow it to cool and serve!

Nutrition:
Calories: 377
Fat: 6.5g
Carbohydrates: 72g
Protein: 10.7g

184. Hot Crunchy Nuts
Preparation Time: 15 minutes
Cooking Time: 35 minutes
Servings: 4
Ingredients:
- 1 cup mixed nuts

- 1 tablespoon melted plant butter
- ¼ teaspoon hot sauce
- ¼ teaspoon garlic powder
- ¼ teaspoon onion powder

Directions:
1. Set the oven to 350 degrees Fahrenheit.
2. Prepare a baking sheet with baking paper.
3. Combine nuts, garlic powder, onion powder, vegan butter, and hot sauce in a medium bowl.
4. On a baking sheet, spread the mixture and toast for 10 minutes.
5. Serve after the nuts have cooled completely.

Nutrition:
Calories: 173.
Protein: 5 g
Fat: 16 g
Carbs: 6 g
Fiber: 3 g

185. Nutty Bites

Preparation Time: 2 minutes
Cooking Time: 0 Minutes
Servings: 6

Ingredients:
- 1 ripe peeled banana
- ¼ cup maple syrup
- ¼ cup melted sunflower seed butter
- 1½ cups quick oats
- 2 teaspoons ground flaxseed
- 1 teaspoon vanilla extract
- ⅓ cup dried unsweetened cranberries
- ¾ cup rolled oats
- ⅓ cup unsweetened vegan protein powder

Directions:
1. Add the banana in a bowl and mash it with a fork.
2. Put in butter and maple syrup and combine until smooth.
3. Next, add protein powder, oats, flaxseed and vanilla extract.
4. Carefully fold in the cranberries.
5. Give a good mix until combined.

6. Make even-sized balls with your hands with the mixture.
7. Arrange the balls in a single layer on a butter paper-lined baking tray.
8. Put it in the fridge to chill before serving.

Nutrition:
Calories: 210
Fat: 7g
Saturated Fat: 1.5g
Trans Fat: 0g
Cholesterol: 0 mg
Sodium: 120mg
Carbohydrates: 34g
Fiber: 4g
Sugars: 17g
Protein; 5g

186. Delicious Greek-style Fruit Compote

Preparation Time: 10 minutes
Cooking Time: 20 minutes
Servings: 4

Ingredients:
- 3 pitted and sliced peaches
- 4 halved and pitted apricots
- 4 dried apricots
- 1 cup dried figs
- 1 cup sweet red wine
- 1 cinnamon stick
- 1 vanilla bean
- 1 cup full-fat coconut yogurt
- 4 tablespoons agave syrup
- 3-4 cloves
- Water

Directions:
1. In a saucepan, add dried fruits, wine, agave syrup, cloves, cinnamon and vanilla.
2. Add enough water
3. Bring the mixture to a boil and reduce the heat immediately to a simmer.
4. Cover it partially and let it simmer for 15 minutes.
5. After letting it cool completely.
6. Ladle into individual bowls and serve with granola.

Nutrition:
Calories: 294
Fat: 1g
Carbs: 66.8g

Protein: 7.8g

187. No-Bake Easy Chocolate Squares
Preparation Time: 10 minutes
Cooking Time: 1 hour 10 minutes
Servings: 20
Ingredients:
- 1 cup cashew butter
- 1 cup almond butter
- ¼ cup melted coconut oil
- ¼ cup raw cacao powder
- 1 teaspoon vanilla paste
- ¼ teaspoon ground cinnamon
- ¼ teaspoon ground cloves
- 2oz. vegan dark chocolate
- 4 tablespoons agave syrup

Directions:
1. Blend all the ingredients in your blender until smooth.
2. Using a spatula, scrape the mixture onto a parchment-lined baking sheet.
3. Let it set in the freezer for an hour.
4. Slice into squares and serve.

Nutrition:
Calories: 187
Fat: 13.8g
Carbs: 15.1g
Protein: 2.9g

188. Vegan Chocolate Mug Cake
Preparation Time: 1 minute
Cooking Time: 1 minute
Servings: 1
Ingredients:
- 2 tablespoons whole-grain flour
- 2 tablespoons cocoa powder
- 2 tablespoons brown sugar
- ⅛ teaspoon sea salt
- 3 tablespoons plant-based milk
- ½ teaspoon pure vanilla extract
- 2 tablespoons dairy free chocolate chips
- ¼ teaspoon baking powder
- 1 tablespoon melted coconut oil

Directions:
1. Take a mug and add all the ingredients. and top with chocolate chips.
2. Put it in the microwave for 40 seconds, or more if you want a firmer center.
3. Serve immediately!

Nutrition:
Calories: 321
Carbohydrates: 44g
Protein: 5g
Fat: 16g
Saturated fat: 2g
Sodium: 317mg
Potassium: 317mg
Fiber: 4g
Sugar: 26g

189. Spiced Apple Chia Pudding
Preparation Time: 20 minutes
Cooking Time: 30 Minutes
Servings : 1
Ingredients:
- ½ cup unsweetened applesauce
- 1 tablespoon chia seeds
- 1½ teaspoons brown sugar
- ¼ cup non-dairy milk
- A pinch of ground cinnamon

Directions:
1. Stir together all the ingredients in a small bowl.
2. Let it sit for half an hour until chia seeds expand and soften.
3. Serve it once it is done!

Nutrition:
Calories 153
Protein: 3g
Fat: 5g
Saturated fat: 1g
Carbohydrates: 26g
Fiber: 10g

190. Chocolate Coconut Macaroons
Preparation Time: 10 minutes
Cooking Time: 25 minutes
Servings: 4
Ingredients:

- 1 cup shredded coconut
- 1 tablespoon vanilla extract
- ⅔ cup coconut milk
- ¼ cup pure maple syrup
- 2 tablespoon cocoa powder
- A pinch of salt

Directions:
1. Turn the oven on to 360 degrees Fahrenheit.
2. In a pot, mix all the ingredients and cook until a steady dough takes form.
3. Use the dough to shape balls with your hand.
4. Place the balls on a baking sheet lined with parchment paper.
5. Bake for 15 minutes.
6. Let cool before serving.

Nutrition:
Calories 180
Total Fat 14g
Saturated Fat 9g
Cholesterol 0 mg
Sodium 50 mg
Carbohydrates 13g
Fiber 4g
Sugars 7g
Protein 3g

191. Chocolate Avocado Ice Cream
Preparation Time: 5 minutes
Cooking Time: 0 minute
Servings: 2

Ingredients:
- 4.5oz. peeled & pitted avocado
- ½ cup unsweetened cocoa powder
- 1 tablespoon unsweetened vanilla extract
- ½ cup & 2 tablespoons maple syrup
- 13.5oz. unsweetened coconut milk
- ½ cup water

Directions:
1. Pulse avocado and milk in a food processor for 2 minutes or until smooth.
2. Put in the rest of the ingredients and blend to combine.
3. Add the mixture to a container and store in the freezer for four hours until firm.
4. Do not forget to whisk every 20 minutes after an hour.

5. Serve once it is firm!

Nutrition:
Calories: 80.7
Fat: 7.1 g
Carbohydrates: 6 g
Protein: 0.6 g
Fiber: 2 g

192. Peanut Nut Butter Maple Dip
Preparation Time: 10 minutes
Cooking Time: 1 hour
Servings: 3

Ingredients:
- ½ tablespoon ground flaxseed
- 1 teaspoon ground cinnamon
- 2 tablespoons cashew milk
- ¾ cups crunchy unsweetened peanut butter
- ½ tablespoon maple syrup

Directions:
1. Combine all the ingredients in a bowl.
2. Stir everything properly by using a fork: the consistency should be creamy.
3. If it is too dry, add a little more milk and peanut butter to loosen the texture.
4. Keep it in the fridge for an hour in a jar before serving.

Nutrition:
Calories: 165
Sugar: 7g
Fat: 12g
Carbohydrates: 9.5g
Fiber: 1g
Protein: 4g

193. Chocolate Oatmeal
Preparation Time: 10 minutes
Cooking Time: 7 minutes
Servings: 1

Ingredients
- 1 cup rolled oats
- 1 cup plant-based milk
- 1 cup water
- ½ teaspoon vanilla extract
- ½ teaspoon cinnamon
- ⅛ teaspoon salt
- 3 tablespoons cocoa powder
- 2 tablespoons maple syrup

Directions:
1. Add all ingredients to a small pot.

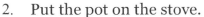

2. Put the pot on the stove.
3. Cook over medium flame until thick and creamy, while also stirring occasionally.
4. It should take around 8 minutes.
5. Mix the oatmeal frequently so it does not stick to the bottom of the pot.
6. Serve oatmeal in a bowl with your favorite topping.

Nutrition:
Calories: 215
Sugar: 7g
Fat: 5g
Saturated Fat: 0.5g
Carbohydrates: 39g
Fiber: 8g
Protein: 7g

194. **Yummy Pumpkin Mug Cake**
Preparation Time: 3 minutes
Cooking Time: 2 minutes
Servings:
Ingredients:
- ¼ cup pumpkin purée
- 3 tablespoons almond milk
- 1 tablespoon almond butter
- 1 tablespoon maple syrup
- ½ teaspoon baking powder
- ¼ teaspoon pumpkin pie spice
- 1 teaspoon vanilla extract
- ½ cup oat flour
- ¼ teaspoon cinnamon
- ⅛ teaspoon salt

Directions:
1. Add all the ingredients to the mug and whisk them.
2. Dry should be added first and wet later.
3. Put the mug in the microwave for 2 minutes.
4. Once done, take it out and serve with your favorite toppings.

Nutrition:
Calories: 410
Sugar: 15g
Fat: 13g

Carbohydrates: 60g
Fiber: 10g
Protein: 15g

195. **Delicious Sautéed Pears**
Preparation Time: 10 minutes
Cooking Time: 35 Minutes
Servings: 6
Ingredients:
- 2 tablespoons vegan butter
- ¼ teaspoon cinnamon
- 1 tablespoon lemon juice
- ½ cup toasted & chopped walnuts
- ¼ teaspoon nutmeg
- 6 peeled & quartered bosc pears

Directions:
1. Add your spices to the butter as it melts in a skillet.
2. Cook for half-minute before adding to the pears.
3. Stir in your lemon juice after cooking for fifteen minutes.
4. Garnish with walnuts if you like.

Nutrition:
Calories: 220
Protein: 2 g
Fat: 10 g
Carbohydrates: 31 g

196. **Tasteful Zucchini Brownies**
Preparation Time: 10 minutes
Cooking time: 45 minutes
Servings: 24
Ingredients:
- 2 cups whole-grain flour
- 1 ½ cups vegan sugar
- 1 teaspoon baking soda
- 1 teaspoon fine sea salt
- 2 tablespoons pure vanilla extract
- ½ cup plant-based oil
- 2 cups peeled & grated zucchini
- ½ cup unsweetened cocoa

Directions:
1. Combine cocoa, salt, flour, sugar and baking soda together.
2. Mix in your oil, vanilla and zucchini. Combine well.

3. Then bake at 350 degrees Fahrenheit in a 9 by 13-inch pan until done.
4. Let it cool before cutting and serving.

Nutrition:
Calories: 138
Protein: 1.5 g
Fat: 4.8 g
Carbohydrates: 21.9 g

197. **Vanilla Rice Pudding**
Preparation Time: 10 minutes
Cooking Time: 1 Hour 35 Minutes
Servings: 6

Ingredients:
- 1 teaspoon pure vanilla extract
- ½ teaspoon fine sea salt
- ½ teaspoon cinnamon
- ¼ teaspoon nutmeg
- 3 tablespoons applesauce
- 3 cups light coconut milk
- 2 cups cooked brown rice

Directions:
1. Pour all of the ingredients into a two-quarter dish after blending them all together.
2. Bake at 300 degrees Fahrenheit for 90 minutes.
3. Serve once when it is cooled.

Nutrition:
Calories: 330
Protein: 5 g
Fat: 10 g
Carbs: 52 g

198. **Vegan Hot Chocolate**
Preparation Time: 5 minutes
Cooking Time: 5 minutes
Servings: 2

Ingredients:
- 2 cups almond milk
- 2 heaping tablespoons cocoa powder
- 2 tablespoons maple syrup
- 2 tablespoons chocolate chips
- 1 teaspoon vanilla extract
- ½ teaspoon ground cinnamon
- A pinch of sea salt

- Marshmallows

Directions:
1. Add everything to a saucepan.
2. Put the saucepan on medium flame, mix the ingredients together, until fully combined and make warm.
3. Do not bring it to a boil.
4. Once warm, pour the hot chocolate into mugs and top with marshmallows

Nutrition:
Calories: 197
Sugar: 22g
Fat: 5g
Carbohydrates: 29g
Fiber: 2g
Protein: 2g

199. **Raspberry Mango Bowl**
Preparation Time: 5 minutes
Cooking Time: 5 minutes
Servings: 2

Ingredients:
- 1 cup frozen mango chunks
- ¾ cup frozen raspberries
- 1 peeled frozen banana
- 1 tablespoon hemp seeds
- 1 cup plant-based milk

Directions:
1. Blend or process all ingredients in a high-speed blender.
2. Make it smooth and creamy, adding more milk if needed.
3. Put smoothie in a bowl and add your favorite toppings.

Nutrition:
Calories: 319
Sugar: 30g
Fat: 8g
Saturated Fat: 0g
Carbohydrates: 60g
Fiber: 12g
Protein: 7g

200. **Apple Pie Bowl**
Preparation Time: 5 minutes
Cooking Time: 5 minutes
Servings: 2

Ingredients:
- 1 cored & chopped red or green apple
- 1 peeled frozen ripe banana
- ¼ cup rolled oats
- 2 pitted "medjool" dates
- ⅛ teaspoon ground ginger
- ⅛ teaspoon ground nutmeg
- ⅓ cup oat milk
- ½ teaspoon vanilla extract
- ½ teaspoon ground cinnamon

Directions:
1. Put all ingredients in the blender.
2. Blend all ingredients until smooth and creamy.
3. Put smoothie in a bowl and serve with your favorite toppings.

Nutrition:
Calories: 200
Fat: 1.5g
Saturated Fat: 0g
Carbohydrates: 48g
Fiber: 7g
Protein: 3g

Chapter 14: 28-Day Meal Plan

Week 1

Breakfast	No.	Lunch	No.	Dinner	No.	Dessert	No.
Yummy Jelly & Peanut Butter Oatmeal		Roasted Vegetables With Granola		Potatoes & Peas Creamy Curry		Vegan Chocolate Mug Cake	
Sweet potatoes with a twist		Bell Peppers With Spinach & Tofu		Vegan Spinach Ricotta		Chocolate Avocado Ice Cream	
Gluten Free Banana Muffins		Tarragon Potato Chips		Simple Scalloped Potatoes		Chocolate Oatmeal	
Nutritional Tofu Scramble		Seitan Bell Pepper Balls		Creamy Turnip Mash		Hazelnut Topped Coconut Caramelized Bananas	
Crunchy Almond Cereal Breakfast		Lentil & Sweet Potato Soup		Healthy Zucchanoush		Coconut Fat Rounds	
Delicious Quinoa & Apple Breakfast Porridge		Cucumber Stuffed Tomatoes		Vegan Super food Bowl		Spiced Apple Chia Pudding	
Healthy Buckwheat Crepes		Cauliflower With Tahini		Nutritious Tofu & Asparagus Stir Fry		Homemade Easy Raisins	

Week 2

Breakfast	No.	Lunch	No.	Dinner	No.	Dessert	No.
Healthy Strawberry & Coconut Smoothie		Flavorful Chickpea Noodle Soup		Healthy Vegetable Chili		No-Bake Easy Chocolate Squares	
Gluten-Free Blueberry Pancakes		Healthy Tomato Barley Soup		Vegetable Kebabs With Coconut Sauce		Chocolate Coconut Macaroons	
Breakfast Chia Seeds Chocolate Pudding		Citrus Kale Salad		Flavorful Black Bean Avocado Tacos		Spiced Apple Chia Pudding	
Fresh Avocado Toast With Pesto		Vegan Yellow Split Peas		Vegetable One Pot Orzo		Nutty Bites	
Red Pepper Hash Browns		Vegan Tuna Salad		The Ultimate Vegetable Stew		Raspberry Mango Bowl	
Banana Cocoa Smoothie		Fried Pineapple Rice		Cabbage & Beet Stew		Vanilla Rice Pudding	
Gluten-Free Chocolate Chip Muffins		Chard Wraps With Millet		Parsley Lemon Pasta		Yummy Pumpkin Mug Cake	

Week 3

Breakfast	No.	Lunch	No.	Dinner	No.	Dessert	No.
Aquafaba French Toast		Coconut parsley wraps		Cauliflower Black Bean Rice		Hot Crunchy Nuts	
Vegan Whole Wheat Waffles		Roasted Sweet Potatoes with Granola		Corn Kernel Black Bean Rice		Delicious Sautéed Pears	
Vegan Chickpea Frittatas		Versatile Garlic Herb Lentils		Potato & Corn Chowder		No-Bake Peanut Butter Oat Bars	
Sweet Potatoes Breakfast Smoothie		Chipotle Whole-Wheat Toast		Tomato Pesto Quinoa		Apple Pie Bowl	
Chia Seed Vanilla Overnight Pudding		Greens & Grains Healthy Bowl		Creamy Mushroom Stroganoff		Tasteful Zucchini Brownies	
Colorful Broiled Grapefruit Breakfast		Versatile Garlic Herb Lentils		Vegan Bean Quesadilla		Lime & Watermel on Granita	
Vegan Strawberr y Banana Milkshake		Lentil Sloppy Joes		Easy Quinoa Sweet Potato Chili		Quick Banana Fritters	

Week 4

Breakfast	No.	Lunch	No.	Dinner	No.	Dessert	No.
Vegetable Tofu Scramble		Avocado Toast With Flaxseeds		Simple & Vegan Mexican Style Rice		Cocoa Almond Energy Bites	
Healthy Smoothie Bowl		Chipotle Sweet Potato Fries		Vegan Adzuki Beans With Rice		Chocolate Coconut Brownies	
Quinoa & Breakfast Patties		Mexican-style Onion Rings		Creamy Curried Potatoes & Peas		Classic Bread Pudding With Sultanas	
Vegetable Panini For Breakfast		Delicata Squash Tahini Fries		Black Bean and Onion Pilaf		Oatmeal Cookies	
Healthy Cinnamon Apples		Creamy Vegan Tofu Bean Tacos		Cashew Cheese Mushroom Pea Farro		Vanilla Mint Ice Cream	
Delicious Quinoa & Apple Breakfast Porridge		Cucumber Stuffed Tomatoes		Vegan Super food Bowl		Spiced Apple Chia Pudding	
Healthy Buckwheat Crepes		Cauliflower With Tahini		Nutritious Tofu & Asparagus Stir Fry		Homemade Easy Raisins	

Chapter: 15 Nutritional Info

No	Plant-Based Protein Sources	(Per 100g).
1.	Seitan	72 g
2.	Nutritional Yeast	52g
3.	Spirulina	57g
4.	Hemp Seeds	31g
5.	Pumpkin Seeds	30g
6.	Lentils	26g
7.	Kidney Beans	24g
8.	Mung Beans	24g
9.	Cannellini Beans	22g
10.	Black Beans	22g
11.	Sunflower Seeds	21g
12.	Almonds	21g
13.	Lime Beans	21g
14.	Chickpeas	19g
15.	Tempeh	19g
16.	Flaxseeds	18g
17.	Sesame Seeds	18g
18.	Chia Seeds	17g

No	Plant-Based Omega-3 Sources	(Per 100g).
1.	Perila Oil	58g
2.	Tofu	0.6g
3.	Hempseed Oil	18g
4.	Beans	0.54g
5.	Hemp Hearts	8.68g
6.	Brussels Sprouts	0.17g
7.	Walnuts	9.3g
8.	Chia Seeds	17.83g
9.	Wild Rice	0.3g
10.	Flaxseeds	22.9g
11.	Seaweed	0.19g
12.	Basil	1.4g

No	Plant-Based Vitamin B12 Sources	(Grams)
1.	Nutritional Yeast (per 100g)	48.7 mcg
2.	Marmite + Yeast Spreads (per 100g)	1.3 mcg
3.	Fortified Soy + Almond Milk (per 100g)	0.4 mcg
4.	Fortified Cereals (per 100g)	3.3 mcg
5.	Rice Milk (1 cup)	240g
6.	Fortified Coconut Milk (1 cup)	240g
7.	Cremini Mushrooms (1 cup)	87g
8.	Portabella Mushroom (1 cup)	86g
9.	White Mushroom (1 cup)	70g
10.	Oat Milk (1 cup)	240g
12.	Acai Berry Juice (1 cup)	266g

Chapter 16: Conversion Charts

CONVERSION CHART

Dry Measurements

CUPS	TABLESPOONS	TEASPOONS	OUNCES	MILLILITERS
1 C.	16 Tbsp.	48 tsp.	8 oz.	237 ml
3/4 C.	12 Tbsp.	36 tsp.	6 oz.	177 ml
2/3 C.	10 & 2/3 Tbsp.	32 tsp.	5 oz.	158 ml
1/2 C.	8 Tbsp.	24 tsp.	4 oz.	118 ml
1/3 C.	5 & 1/3 Tbsp.	16 tsp.	3 oz.	79 ml
1 / 4 C.	4 Tbsp.	12 tsp.	2 oz.	59 ml
1 / 4 C.	2 Tbsp.	6 tsp.	1 oz.	30 ml
1 / 16 C.	1 Tbsp.	3 tsp.	1/2 oz.	15 ml

CONVERSION CHART

Fluid Measurements

GALLON	QUARTS	PINTS	CUPS	OUNCES	LITERS
1 gallon	4 quarts	8 pints	16 cups	128 oz.	3.8 Liters
1/2 gallon	2 quarts	4 pints	8 cups	64 oz.	1.9 Liters
1/4 gallon	1 quart	2 pints	4 cups	32 oz.	95 Liters
---	1/2 quart	1 pints	2 cups	16 oz.	480 ml
---	---	1/2 pints	1 cup	8 oz.	240 ml
---	---	---	1/2 cup	4 oz.	120 ml
---	---	---	1/4 cup	2 oz.	60 ml
---	---	---	---	1 oz.	30 ml

OVEN TEMPERATURES

FAHRENHEIT (F)	CELSIUS (C)
250° F	120° C
300° F	150° C
325° F	180° C
375° F	190° C
400° F	200° C
425° F	220° C
450° F	230° C

Conclusion

Now you have everything you need to start a plant-based diet. A collection of basic and simple, healthy plant-based recipes is included in the book, as is a shopping list and a 28-day meal plan that is designed to help you in the beginning.

As with all diet plans, once you master the basics, moving forward is straightforward.

If you have the right guide to take you by the hand and help you through everything and give advice on how to keep temptation at bay, switching to a plant-based diet can be quite simple.

If you want to achieve your health goals, just remember to stick with the plan. Before starting, always clean your kitchen, follow a healthy lifestyle, eat more greens and fruits, and learn to reduce animal consumption entirely.

Pick foods that are high-quality, are more meaningful, and better for your health.

Make the most of our cookbook and prepare some amazing recipes. They can help you stay healthy, wealthy and wise. Good luck on your plant-based diet journey!

Made in the USA
Monee, IL
12 February 2022